SURVIVING
YOUR
ORGANIZATION

Phil Baguley

TEACH YOURSELF BOOKS

For UK order queries: please contact Bookpoint Ltd, 130 Milton Park, Abingdon, Oxon OX14 48B. Telephone: (44) 01235 827720. Fax: (44) 01235 400454. Lines are open from 9.00–18.00, Monday to Saturday, with a 24-hour message answering service. Email address: orders@bookpoint.co.uk

For U.S.A. order queries: please contact McGraw-Hill Customer Services, P.O. Box 545, Blacklick, OH 43004-0545, U.S.A. Telephone: 1-800-722-4726. Fax: 1-614-755-5645.

For Canada order queries: please contact McGraw-Hill Ryerson Ltd., 300 Water St, Whitby, Ontario L1N 9B6, Canada. Telephone: 905 430 5000. Fax: 905 430 5020.

Long renowned as the authoritative source for self-guided learning – with more than 30 million copies sold worldwide – the *Teach Yourself* series includes over 300 titles in the fields of languages, crafts, hobbies, business and education.

British Library Cataloguing in Publication Data
A catalogue record for this title is available from The British Library.

Library of Congress Catalog Card Number: On file

First published in UK 2001 by Hodder Headline Plc, 338 Euston Road, London, NW1 3BH.

First published in US 2001 by Contemporary Books, A Division of The McGraw-Hill Companies, 4255 West Touhy Avenue, Lincolnwood (Chicago), Illinois 60712–1975 U.S.A.

The 'Teach Yourself' name and logo are registered trade marks of Hodder & Stoughton Ltd.

Typeset by Transet Limited, Coventry, England.
Printed in Great Britain for Hodder & Stoughton Educational, a division of Hodder Headline Plc, 338 Euston Road, London NW1 3BH by Cox & Wyman Ltd, Reading, Berkshire.

Impression number   10 9 8 7 6 5 4 3 2 1
Year   2007 2006 2005 2004 2003 2002 2001

BEGIN HERE...

This book starts from the fact that Monday mornings – for most of you – aren't good. The reason for this isn't complicated – it's really quite simple and straightforward. You feel like this because you *don't* want to go back to work – back into the organization that you work for. The aim of this book is to do something about this. It's a book that's about helping you to survive your organization. Doing that isn't anything like as straightforward or as easy as it used to be. Nowadays, the household names of the marketplace – the ones that we've relied upon for decades – falter and fall in the face of global waves of change. In their place we get organizations that explode, in months, from being an idea on the back of a pizza delivery box to having a turnover twice that of most African states.

All this means that surviving your organization isn't just yet another challenging task. It's *the* task for you. It's a task that demands skill, courage and dedication. Copping-out, keeping your head below the line of fire and popping up to grab what you can from time to time is no longer a realistic option. But, in the face of the whirlwind of change that we're all coming to recognize as our new millennium, it would be just as unrealistic or impractical if this was one of those 'do it by numbers' or '12 step' guides. For *your* survival is individual to *you*. It will depend upon *your* skill, *your* ability and *your* wisdom. All of which means that this isn't just a book that's aimed at helping you to survive – it's also a book about *your* growth and *your* development.

By now you should be getting the message about what this book is about. You should also, just as importantly, be getting a message about what it's *not* about. But let's try to make that a little clearer. It's *not* a book about perpetuating the old myths – the ones like '*bosses have a divine right to rule*' or '*bosses know better than anybody else*'. Nor is it about ideas that tell you that working in an organization is always a serious, heavy-duty business or that the key to success in your organization lies in unquestioning conformity and unchallenging obedience. If those are close to the way you see it, then it's probably better and certainly safer if you bail out now, before it gets too late and you catch a glimpse of a different way of being and seeing. For the remainder of you – those of you who have enough spirit, courage, verve and sense of freedom to want to create an organization fit for people – then, this is *the* book for you.

CORE VALUES

Before you go any further you need to look at some of the basic stuff. That is you need to grasp and come to terms with the fact that built into this book are some important core values. There are five of these – five beliefs/value statements. Everything else in the book reflects these. So getting hold of these values, achieving an early sync with them isn't just important – it's *vital* if this book is going to help you. So, here they are:

■ Organizations are *people* – not machines or systems or office blocks or factories – but *people*
■ These *people* matter – all of them
■ These *people* don't go to work just for money
■ These *people* want to be able to enjoy their work
■ These *people* are key to the survival and success of all organizations

There are very few of us who would *not* sign up to these. They seem to be woven into the fabric of our common culture, irrespective of creed, nation or occupation. They are core values that spring up, unbidden, wherever and whenever organizations exist. Their presence here should begin to tell you that this is no ordinary 'teach yourself' book. For it's *the* book for those of you who want to make a shift in your working lives. That's the shift from where work is a four letter word to where your work becomes interesting, stimulating, even fun. This shift will be key to the rest of your working life – it'll transform what you do at work and the way that you do it. This book is designed to help you make that change. It draws from a wide and eclectic range of sources – all of which make the common statement: that the people of our organizations matter. It also aims to provoke, question and challenge you; it asks you to look again at the fallacies, stupidities and follies that the decades, even the centuries, have built into your organization.

WHY?

By now, some of you might be beginning to wonder what this is all about. 'Why rock the boat,' you might be saying to yourself, 'I've done all right so far'. One part of the answer is that – for all of us – time is running out. None of our individual beliefs, hopes and desires have infinite shelf lives. The other part of the answer lies in the fact that whenever you come up against something in your life that challenges your beliefs, hopes and desires you face a difficult choice. You can either give up a part of your dreams and hopes and acquiesce to how others think that you ought to be or you can use that pressure, that challenge, to refine and strengthen your wish to be yourself.

This book is about the second of these alternatives – that of standing by what you believe in. It's not an easy option; it's one that requires courage, strength, patience and determination. But it's also, above all, an act of self-determination and self-empowerment. It takes the 'r' out of revolution and turns it into evolution. But here, if you're still puzzled, are some of the reasons that other people have given:

'So that working here is more fun.'

'So that when I go home at night I feel that I've done something worthwhile.'

'So I get listened to – occasionally.'

'So that we do things better.'

'Wouldn't it be nice ...'

So what are your reasons? There'll be more than one; most people have four or five. Write yours down in the box on the next page – if you dare! But if you're not yet ready to do that, then don't give up. Be patient with yourself, and this book. Turn the page, go to the next section and then take a look at the Contents list on pages 6–8. If that doesn't work then have a browse around. Take a chance – pick a section at random and see where it takes you – but don't forget to come back and fill in the box!

> 'Going to work for a large company is like getting on a train. Are you doing sixty miles an hour or is the train doing sixty miles an hour and you're just sitting still?'
> J. Paul Getty

MY REASONS

I want to change the way things are done in my organization because:

1

2

3

4

5

HOW TO USE THIS BOOK

If you're going to use this book and do that to good effect in your working life then you're going to need to:

■ find your way around the book quickly and easily, and then
■ use what you find there.

We've done quite a lot about the first of these. The result is a book that's different. It's structured and written so you can easily access its contents and read, understand and absorb any one of its sections within ten minutes. But these sections are very different from those you may find in other books. Arranged in alphabetical order, each section starts a new page and focuses on an aspect of life in an organization. Sprinkled amongst them are 'How Not To' case studies and cartoons – each with a message. All of these are listed in the Contents section which follows this page.

This means that you can read it in whichever way you want to. You can be logical, linear, alphabetic, intuitive, impulsive or crazy – it's up to you. However you do it, what you'll find here will lead you to start questioning the basic assumptions that you make about organizations and the ways that we all behave in them.

So how do you use all this to help you survive in your organization? This is easier than you might think. You start by removing the blinkers that you're wearing. Then you look around the organization that you're working in. What you'll see – maybe even fall over – are the sorts of nonsenses and idiocies that are built into the systems of *all* organizations. They're the 'we've always done it this way' or the 'this suits us, so why should we change?' attitudes that we all know about – the ones that limit the efficiency of you and your co-workers and stop you giving your customers the service they deserve. After a while you'll get the knack of spotting them. After all, if you're any good at your job you've probably been finding ways to get around them for quite some time before you picked up this book. But spotting these isn't going to be enough, as you'll see later. You'll want to do something about them – and that will involve other people and take time and patience. After a while you'll find that looking at things in this way becomes a habit. Soon, you'll find that you've changed. Amongst other things, you'll be finding it easier to get out of bed to come to work on a Monday morning.

6 CONTENTS

A

As, Bs and Cs 9
Abuse 10
Acronyms 11
Adaptability 12
Ageism 13
Aggression 14
Anachronisms 16
Archaeology – Corporate 17
Assertion 18

B

Betrayal 19
Black Bag Days 20
Blame 21
Bosses – Good 23
Bosses – New 24
Bosses – Not So Good 25
Bosses – Terrible 27
Bull 28
Bullying 29
Buzzwords 31

C

Call Yourself Up 32
Caring 33
Change 34
Communication 36
Compassion 38
Competition 39
Compromise 40
Consensus 41
Conversations 42
Courage 44
Customers 45

D

Decisions 46
Delegation 48

Dialogues and Discussions 49
Disobedience 50
Dominance 51
Downsizing 52
Dressing Up and Dressing Down 54
Duvet Days 55

E

E-mail 56
Eccentricity 58
Efficiency and Effectiveness 59
Empathy 61
Empowerment 62
Enjoyment 64
Excellence 65

F

Feedback 67
Flexibility 69
Freaks – Control and Other 70
Friends 72

G

Games 73
Glass Ceilings 74
Go – No-Go 76
Good – and Bad – Hair Days 77
Gossip 78
Grapevines 79
Gurus 80

H

Harassment 82
Hope 84
How Not To No. 1 –
    The Interview 32
How Not To No. 2 – People Care 47
How Not To No. 3 –
    Persuasion 53

How Not To No. 4 – The E-mail   60
How Not To No. 5 – More People
   Care   83
How Not To No. 6 – The Plan   105
How Not To No. 7 – Customer
   Care   130
How Not To No. 8 – People
   Management   146
How Not To No. 9 – New Broom
   Strikes Out   173
How Not To No. 10 – Motivation
   and Performance   181

I
Incredible Shrinking Chips   85
Influence – or Power?   86
Institutionalization   88

J
Jack of All Trades   90
Jargon   91
Job Titles   92

K
Knowledge Worker   93

L
Lateral Thinking   94
Laughter   95
Leadership 1   96
Leadership 2   97
Listening   98
Loyalty   100
Luck   101

M
Management   102
Management Consultants 1   103
Management Consultants 2   104
Meetings   107
Mind and Body   109
Miracles   111
Mistakes   112
Moaning   113

Monologues and Chats   114

N
Negotiating   115
Networking   117
New   118
Norms   119
Nose to Nose   120

O
Office Politics   122
Office Romances   123
Organizations   124

P
Pecking Order   127
People   128
Persuasion   131
Planning   133
Prejudice   134
Projects   135
Promises   136

Q
Quality   137
Quick – or Slow ?   139
Quiet   140

R
Racism   142
Reasons To Be Cheerful   144
Re-invention   145
Relaxez-Vous   147
Résumés and Other Stories   148
Risk   149

S
Secondments   151
Secrets   153
Self Stuff   155
Silent Majorities   156
Singing   157
Stakeholders   158
Staying Healthy   159

8

Storytellers 160
Success 161

T
Tall Poppies 162
Teams 163
Testing Times 165
Thirty-Five Plus 167
Times a'wasting 169
To Boldly Go 170
Tolerance 172
Training 174
Trust 177

U
Unwritten Rules 178

V
Vacations 180
Vindictiveness 182

W
Waves, Smiles and Frowns 183
We're Going To Have To
 Let You Go 184
What Makes Us Work The Way
 We Do? 186
Whistle-blowing 187
Who Cares? 189
Winding Up and Winding Down 190
Write Words 192

X
Xeroxing – or Me Too 193

Y
Yakkity-Yak 194
You're In – or You're Out 196
Your Future 197

Z
Zany 199
Zen 200

As, Bs AND Cs

The alphabet soup that you find in your organization (*see* **Acronyms**) isn't new. When the economist Vilfredo Pareto studied the distribution of income in late nineteenth century Italy, he found what we now call the ABC or 80:20 rule – Pareto's Principle. He discovered that the significant items in any group are in the minority – 'the vital few' – and the majority of the group are relatively unimportant – 'the trivial many'. This sort of division applies to many other situations. The proportions of these 'few' and 'many' will vary, but the principle won't. You'll find, for example, that 90, 80 or 70 per cent of your stock value, or assembly costs comes from 10, 20 or 30 per cent of your stock items held, or components used.

The alphabet soup or ABC version of the Pareto Principle ranks inventory into three classes – A, B and C – and then focuses your attention on the Class A items. These, of course, are the 20 per cent of your inventory items that account for 80 per cent of the movements in and out of that inventory.

So how does this affect your survival and growth in your organization? The answer, if you think about it, is almost as obvious as ABC. For 90, 80 or 70 per cent of your problems or pleasures come from 10, 20 or 30 per cent of the things that you do, or people that you meet.

Use the Pareto Principle – with care and skill – and it will help you to identify, and be clearer about, those things or people that 'get up your nose' or limit the pleasure that you get out of being at work. It'll also help you to find and focus on those things or people you get a 'kick out of'– that give you most of your pleasure and enjoyment. Then you can get on with either eliminating or building up those key factors. As a result, the efforts that you put into surviving your organization will be more effective – maximum gain for minimum effort – and your survival rating will increase.

Abuse occurs when you misuse something or when you use it wrongly or improperly. It can happen to things and it can happen to people and when it does it leads to these being damaged, used up or worn out. Abuse is actually quite common in organizations.

But it's not the major, significant, abuse that we read about in our newspapers or see on our TV screens. It's usually subtle and insidious rather than in-your-face. Nevertheless you're abused when your organization expects you to carry out your job with inadequate resources or training (*see* **Training**) and then sacks you (*see* **We're Going To Have To Let You Go**) or puts you into disciplinary procedure when you fail to achieve. Organizational abuse rears its ugly head when you're regularly expected to work unpaid overtime and not given time off in lieu. It walks into your working life when you are told to manage the unmanageable (*see* **Delegation**) and penalized when you can't. This organizational abuse often appears in our working lives alongside harassment (*see* **Harassment**), bullying (*see* **Bullying**) or domination (*see* **Dominance**). Just think about it; you'll soon realize that it's much more common than you'd realized.

Dealing with organizational abuse isn't easy. It's usually deeply embedded in the culture of the organization. It's a part of the 'this-is-the-way-we-do-things-around-here' that's been there for a long time. Challenging it is scary. The response you'll get will be dismissive and may even be one of the 'if-you-don't-like-it-then-go' variety. But challenge it you must. For this sort of abuse is fundamentally wrong; it's an improper and incorrect use of an organization's greatest asset – its people. But that's not all it is. For it's also bad for you. It stresses you and makes you inefficient (*see* **Winding Up and Winding Down**; **Efficiency and Effectiveness**). You'll become unhappy and unenthusiastic about coming to work. The choice you face is whether to stand up to and reject that abuse or to put up with it. Before you decide which of these you're going to do, just reflect on the fact that studies of abused children tell us that abuse can lead to abuse. That is when the abused learn how to abuse others. Whether you do that – abuse others – is, of course, up to you. But before you decide, think about whether you really want to be an abuser.

ACRONYMS

When you look closer at your organization's alphabet soup what you'll find are acronyms. These are, of course, pronounceable words composed of the initial letters of other words. But these – like Pitman's Shorthand or Latin phrases such as 'ad hoc' – aren't a lot of use unless you know what they mean. But the pages of our newspapers and magazines are full of them. There's NATO (North Atlantic Treaty Organisation), RADAR (Radio Detecting and Ranging), PAL (Phase Alternating Line) and RAM (Random Access Memory). Within your organization acronyms usually take the form of a TLA or an FLA – three and four letter acronyms. Inventory control people talk about FIFO (first in first out), operations people talk about JIT (Just in Time) and personnel people talk about HRM (Human Resources Management). Technology has given us acronyms such as http (hypertext transfer protocol), ISDN (integrated services digital network) and ADSL (asymmetric digital subscriber line). Your e-mail (*see* **E-mail**) and web sites are littered with acronyms such as FWIW (for what its worth), FAQ (frequently asked questions) and ATB (all the best).

All of these acronyms were created either because someone thought that they would improve the way you communicate, or alternatively and more likely, because somebody thought that it was a clever way of talking. But what happens when you use an acronym is that you downgrade your communications (*see* **Communication**) and you jargonize the obvious or simple (*see* **Jargon**), thus inhibiting its effectiveness. When this happens you've created a knowledge barrier between you and the person that you're talking to. This is a barrier that defines an in-group – those who use and *sometimes* understand the acronym – and an out-group – comprising those who don't understand what the other group is talking about (*see* **You're In – or You're Out**). None of this helps your communication. Nor does it contribute to the acceptance and use of the idea behind the acronym. So, try to limit your use of acronyms and when you do use them make sure that:

- you really understand what they mean, and
- everybody else also understands what they mean, in real and practical terms.

ADAPTABILITY

Adaptability, *real* adaptability, is something rather special. When it happens you go beyond mere efficiency and effectiveness (*see* **Efficiency and Effectiveness**) and you're able to answer the individual and special needs of your customers (*see* **Customers**). Being adaptable doesn't just add to your survival rating, it also gives you the potential to turn a disgruntled and disappointed customer into a friend for life and a frustrated and anxious co-worker into someone who will climb the nearest mountain for you, if only you'd ask him or her. Adaptability gives us the legends of good customer service: the hotel that remembers that when you last stayed there you asked for an early morning call and a certain newspaper; the mail order outlet that rush delivers that crucial bit of hardware at no extra cost because your computer is off-line until you get it.

But adaptability is rare and organizations that foster it are few and far between. For doing that means giving you the power and authority to respond – directly and without reference to the boss – to each customer's needs. It means trusting you not to abuse or misuse that power and authority and it demands systems which are flexible enough to cope with this adaptability. Above all, it means placing the needs of the customer ahead of the organization's own need for order and predictability. If your organization or work group is adaptable it will delight and captivate your customers. But if it isn't, it won't just disappoint those customers, they won't come back. But even if your organization hasn't yet reached the high peaks of adaptability, there's still a lot that you can do on your own. Check out how adaptable you are by asking yourself how many times in the last 30 days you've 'gone that extra mile' for a customer. If you haven't – why not? If you have – why not more often? The choice is yours. Either you can be known as a responsive person who is interested in the individual needs of your customers, or you can go on being one of those boring 'sorry-we-don't-stock-that' people. If you supervise people you can choose whether you encourage them to be adaptable or whether you want them to keep on referring stuff back to you. It's up to you!

AGEISM

Ageism is the name that's now given to what happens when the young push the not-so-young aside in their haste to claim what they see as their birthright. But this 'get-out-of-my-way,-it's-my-turn-now' stuff isn't new – it's been happening for a long time. What is new is the age that this now kicks in at. It used to be that you could be pretty sure that you'd be useful in the workplace until you reached 60 or 65 years of age. Then it fell to 40 or 45 years of age. These days it's reached the grand old age of 35 (*see* **Thirty-Five Plus**). All of this reflects the recent fashion that puts the young at centre stage. It contains echoes of the Eskimos – who put their old people out on the ice when they can no longer contribute to the family's survival. It also presumes that being young is good and being old is bad. It subscribes to such sweeping generalities as: youth = energy, vitality, creativity, willingness to change and 'good' ideas; and old = worn-out ideas, resistance to change, low levels of energy and creativity.

How you react to all this will, in part, depend on how old you are or, to put it another way, how close you are to the age barrier. But even the most prejudiced (*see* **Prejudice**) will admit that, in reality, it's not really a question of age. It's really about individuality or, to be more precise, attitude. Some are born with the attitudes of old age and hold fast to them throughout their lives, while others stay young until they die. Some show the early

> *'The old age of an eagle is better than the youth of a sparrow.'*
> Greek proverb

symptoms of inflexibility and rigidity in childhood while others revel and delight in the 'new' for all of their lives. But, unfortunately, these observations seem to be having trouble reaching those who do the hiring and firing for our organizations. Despite the research that says that mixed age groups have higher levels of motivation and commitment and lower staff turnover and absenteeism rates, these hirers-and-firers still seem locked into the criticality of your age. Surviving in this sort of environment means accepting that your retirement will be sooner than you thought and planning to allow for that (*see* **Your Future**). But don't forget that things can and do change. For ageism may soon reach the end of its life-span. The older are increasing in number and the economic clout of grey-power has begun to emerge.

These days rage is literally 'all the rage'. Examples include road rage, airline rage, shopping trolley rage and bargain sale rage, to name but a few. These are all examples of the sort of 'aggressive' behaviour, which comes about when you or I don't get or can't have what we want. We get frustrated and then we get angry. But anger is a feeling, while aggression involves actions. These actions are usually aimed at a specific outcome – such as getting rid of an annoyance, getting something or even hurting somebody. Most of the time these feelings are under control but when that control fails we are said to 'be in a rage'.

But the frustration that leads to aggression isn't an instant 'jack-in-a-box' event. It develops slowly, accumulating over a period of time, until, finally, you 'get mad'. During this build-up you often show what you are feeling. These displays are, at first, indirect: you throw yourself into activities that are aimed at distracting you – such as exercising or tidying up, you drink or eat more than usual, you feel 'low' or even guilty and you don't want to talk with other people. When you do talk you say things like 'Why does this always happen to me?' or 'I feel bad all the time'. As the frustration continues, your growing anger begins to show itself. You begin to behave in ways that are sceptical, argumentative and uncooperative; you say things like 'Don't push me, I'll do it when I'm good and ready!' or 'Don't make me laugh'. As the frustration continues your anger begins to show itself more clearly. You start to gossip maliciously (*see* **Gossip**), you become overly critical of others and you show your prejudices (*see* **Prejudice**). At this point your aggression is very close to becoming physical. When this happens doors are slammed and 'phones banged down. Fortunately, in most of our organizations, this rarely escalates into people being pushed, shoved, poked or even hit. What you are expected to put up with are acts of aggression that are aimed at inflicting psychological, rather than physical, harm (*see* **Bullying**). Even so, this form of aggression also has a strong physical element, involving clenched fists and facial expressions such as glaring and frowning.

But do you have to put up with this or any other sort of aggression? The answer is, of course, *No* – you don't have to put up with it. The frustration that leads to aggression is understandable, even acceptable – given the ways and means of our organizations – but the aggression itself is not.

Here are some of the ways that you can survive the sort of aggression that's all too common in our organizations:

1 Recognize it early – in both yourself and others.

2 If it's a 'sniping' sort of aggression, confront the aggressor, get the issue out in the open.

3 If the aggressor is a 'steamroller' who gets his or her way by riding over everybody else's rights, don't confront them directly – wait until they've calmed down. Then approach them and, assertively, express your point of view (*see* **Assertion**).

4 If the aggressor is an 'exploder', wait until the dust settles then tackle them as for the 'steamroller' above.

5 Always deal with aggressors fairly, listen to them, accept the way they feel, try to find ways of working together that you can both live with.

6 Always set limits to violence. Tell them you want to work it out but they need to control their anger.

7 If someone is seriously threatening you, take no chances, take steps to protect yourself immediately.

8 Avoid responding to aggression with aggression. Aggression does not lead to real victory – it merely begets more aggression and that, in its turn, leads to a situation in which nobody wins and all lose.

'Let me know when you've finished.'

| **ANACHRONISMS**

The Chinese language is rich in proverbs. The one we're interested in right now is the one that tells us that when we forget our ancestors we become like 'trees without roots'. A tree like this isn't going to be very successful. It won't get the nourishment that it needs in order to grow and it will probably fall over when the strong winds of winter come along. On the other hand, when a tree grows roots that are *too* big or strong it becomes 'root bound'. This means that the tree becomes, literally, bound or held by its roots. In this condition the tree's growth becomes more and more limited and it becomes less and less productive, generating fewer flowers or fruits.

But it isn't really a horticultural question that you're looking at here – it's actually about what, if anything, your forebears can contribute to your survival – and success – in your organization. People's answers to this question fall into one of two groups. Some will tell you that it's a brave new world that owes nothing to the past. They say that those who went before you are anachronisms, out of place, out of time and out of harmony with the present. Others will say that continuity with your forebears is important and that without the past you'd be nothing (*see* **Storytellers**). The truth, of course, lies between these extremes.

For the knowledge that these 'anachronisms' leave you is relevant. Without it you'd have to rediscover a whole set of basics; with it your exploration of the future has a solid launch pad. But when you look at that knowledge in the cold light of the dawn you'll soon see that the original relevance or applicability of much of it is no longer valid. This is because it's often 'of its time' – and that time has passed. But, before you throw the baby out with the bathwater, let's just acknowledge that, amongst all this there is something of value. Accessing it and using it requires hard work. You need to be able to transpose it into your time, to renegotiate its relevance to your world and to relearn its use. But when you've done that you'll find that these anachronisms have, at their core, pearls of real value; pearls that help you survive in your organization. Amongst these are adaptability (*see* **Adaptability**), caring (*see* **Caring**), compassion (*see* **Compassion**), courage (*see* **Courage**) – and others.

ARCHAEOLOGY – CORPORATE

Archaeology is about ancient history – and that is what most of your organization's culture is about. This word 'culture' is one of the most misused words in the lexicon of business. It's often used incorrectly – to describe (or justify) expediency, prejudice or bigotry or even incompetence. How different these are to the *Oxford English Dictionary*'s definition of culture as 'the intellectual side of civilization'! But in any real or pragmatic sense, the culture of an organization is about the way things are done. This means that it's about choices between Honesty and Deceit, Plain Dealing and Deviousness, Rule by principle and Rule by 'wolf pack', and 'Do as I say' and 'Do as I do'. Some of our organizations have cultures that are obsessed with things like wearing suits and ties while in other organizations the cultural focus is on avoiding conflict at all costs or avoiding individual decision taking and responsibility – by hiding under the blanket of 'consensus' (*see* **Consensus**). However it shows itself, this culture is about the past – the archaeology of the organization. Its roots run down, deep into buried strata of beliefs and stories (*see* **Storytellers**) about the way things used to be done. But, with the passage of time, this folk history of past triumphs and failures often degrades into ritual. It becomes a 'that's the way things are done around here' litany that, over time, has drifted away from reality and become increasingly meaningless. When this happens (and it often does) culture acts as a prison or a strait-jacket. It

> *'I define culture as the collective mental programming of people in an environment.'*
>
> Geert Hofstede

limits, even strangles, our attempts to be the sort of people who do great things for the organization in which we work. Some of us find all this comforting – just as, when babies, we found comfort in being swaddled or wrapped in a blanket. But for others, the view is that the dust and debris of history – disguised as culture – often suffocates innovation and enterprise and that there is no gain without risk (*see* **Risk**).

Take a look at the culture of your organization, check out whether you or your co-workers are being stopped or held back because 'we don't do it that way around here'. If you are, then perhaps it's time for one of you to become a legend in your own time – and so begin to change the culture of your organization.

> *'Culture is an instrument wielded by professors to manufacture professors, who when their turn comes will manufacture professors.'*
>
> Simone Weil

ASSERTION

If you've ever had to walk away from a difficult situation or felt that your rights had been ignored – then assertion can help you. Being assertive is about being effective in your communications and constructive in the way that you get your needs answered. It's about being equal. But assertion often gets a bad press. It's often seen as an act of aggression (*see* **Aggression**) or a tactic that's based on trumpeting your own rights at the expense of those of other people. But, in reality, being assertive is very different from these. Being assertive means expressing your feelings clearly in a way that's respectful to others. There's no domination (*see* **Dominance**) or shouting others down. Nor is it about the opposite – being passive. This means accepting that other people's needs, views and rights are more important than yours. People who act in this way never get their needs answered because they're too busy answering other people's needs. So if assertion isn't about being aggressive or being passive, then what is it about? If you look at the ways you behave as a spectrum with aggression and passivity at opposite ends then, in the middle, you'll find assertion. Here's an example:

Situation	Passive Response	Assertive Response	Aggressive Response
A colleague is openly and unfairly critical of you in a meeting with your boss.	Say nothing and allow your boss to think that the criticism is valid.	Tell your colleague that you are surprised by the comments and would like to discuss his or her feelings at a more appropriate time.	Tell your colleague that he or she doesn't know what he or she is talking about and should shut up!

When you're assertive you stand up for your own rights and say what you want to say about your needs and values. You stand firm at the boundaries of your rights and your personal space. You do not trespass on the rights or space of others. Real assertion releases positive energy. It's an act of self-determination and self-empowerment – one that will increase your survival rating by leaps and bounds (*see* **Empowerment**).

BETRAYAL

Betrayal, and its close cousin, the back-stab, are all-too-familiar aspects of life in the organization. They both have their roots in the dark side of our natures. They are covert and furtive. They conceal themselves behind the trust that you place in those with whom you work. When that trust is broken, when somebody reveals a secret that you shared with them, you feel the pain of that betrayal (*see* **Secrets**). When these happen, you, the betrayed, are usually the last to know. So why then, since it's such a common event, does betrayal always surprise you? The reason for this is simple and obvious – you don't look for it. You don't do this firstly because you trust the people that you work with – you've built up a relationship with them, gradually, and over a period of time. The second reason is that you don't like *not* trusting people – being continually 'on-your-guard' is stressful. So when somebody you trust breaks a confidence – you feel hurt and betrayed. That hurt is about loss. What you've lost is trust, safety and predictability. You also almost always lose the relationship that you thought you had with your betrayer. You might even lose your reputation or your job.

> *'God defend me from my friends, from my enemies I can defend myself.'*
>
> Proverb

But if you're going to survive all this and go on to use the experience to increase your survival rating then there are some key steps that you must take. First, you must accept the loss involved. Second, you must get back on the horse that you just fell off – find someone that you trust to talk to about it, preferably a good listener (*see* **Listening**). The third step is to be patient with yourself. After all, grieving over any loss takes time. The fourth and last step is to make sure that you learn from your betrayal. Use it to learn how to trust (*see* **Trust**) with more discrimination. Use it to look at the organization you work in, to see how it did – or didn't – support you or whether it accepted the betrayal. In the end, there's only one fail-safe way to avoid betrayal and that is to stop trusting people. But, if you decide to do that, remember that, trust is the lubricating oil of our organizations. Without it, they – and you – will be unable to move forward.

BLACK BAG DAYS

Everybody has Black Bag Days. They're the days when you look at the large and growing pile of papers on your desk and feel an irresistible urge to sweep them all into a large black plastic bag and away down to the shredder. They're the days when you open your e-mail file and find that you've still not had an answer – or at least one that makes sense – to all those urgent e-mails that you sent so long ago and your finger hovers over the 'delete' button. They are the days when the pile of uncertainties becomes too large, too wide and too heavy for you to hold it together. They're the days when that pile of unfinished business – the one that's such a part of 'life' in your organization – goes unstable, falls over and becomes redundant.

It only takes a small movement, a flick of the wrist, a click on 'delete', and that particular pile of history will fall off your desk or out of your computer and into whatever black bag you have to hand. Yet most of you hesitate, you hold back at the brink, you hang on to your history hoping that it will make tomorrow more certain. But it doesn't, does it? For Black Bag Days are a natural phenomenon. They are the days when the redundancy that's built into most natural systems rises to the surface, the days the leaves fall off your particular 'tree'. Fighting it doesn't do any good. In fact, it makes it worse. The more you struggle to keep your 'finger in the hole in the dyke' or to 'hold it together' then the higher the drive to degrade rises. Better, by far, to give in, to allow the slide into the black plastic bag.

But doing this gracefully, and, above all, doing it before you yourself are drawn into the gaping mouth of that black bag is a real survival skill. It takes good timing and real nerve. These are the skills that will enable you to clear your desk and your computer's e-mail file of all that redundant 'history'. But that's not all they'll do. You'll find that they will also get rid of all those redundant feelings that you carry around with you – all the unspoken 'sorry's', 'how-dare-you's' and 'no's' of your past. Then – at the end of your Black Bag Day – you'll be ready to stake a claim to a new future.

BLAME

Blame is one of those words – like vindictiveness (*see* **Vindictiveness**) or racism (*see* **Racism**) – that are fundamentally negative. It's a word that's coloured with censure and disapproval; it's one that often leads to discipline or demerit. The three Rs – reproach, rebuke and reprimand – follow in blame's train. Blame usually gets allocated when things go 'wrong'. When that happens we usually have to find somebody – or something – to 'put the blame on to'. So we blame somebody or something that we think is responsible for whatever has happened, hoping to make them answerable for that wrong.

Few of our organizations are blame-free. It seems to be a part of a culture that's common to them all. Someone has to 'carry the can' when things go wrong. But in some, the use – or

> '*Blame is safer than praise.*'
> Waldo Emerson

rather, the misuse – of blame takes a step further. In these organizations blaming is a 'must-do' action. The need to blame lies deep within their culture (*see* **Archaeology – Corporate**). These organizations expend a lot of energy (and money) in defining what is 'wrong' and what is 'right', usually in the form of checklists, standards, procedures or schedules. While these may appear to be for your guidance, they're actually not. They are really about the things that you must and must not do. Get these wrong and you'll suffer the consequences – usually in the form of disciplinary procedures or the sack (*see* **We're Going To Have To Let You Go**). The need to do this is so strong in some managers that they'll even resort to 'drawing a line in the sand' or an informal and 'off-the-record' warning (*see* **Harassment**) for alleged minor mistakes (*see* **Mistakes**). All of this, of course, leads to a workplace in which mistakes are covered up and hidden – rather than acknowledged and owned. It creates workplaces in which blame and punishment are the norms (*see* **Norms**) – rather than support, constructive examination and learning. Control freaks (*see* **Freaks – Control and Other**) thrive in this sort of organization. They love to define what's 'right' or what's 'wrong', what's 'good' or what's 'bad' and, of course, to decide who's to blame in what they call investigations, audits or post mortems.

If you're not sure whether you do or don't work in a blame organization then try the following check-list.

TO BLAME OR NOT TO BLAME

Ask yourself the following questions – and answer them honestly:

- ■ Do your co-workers and bosses accept mistakes and failure? ❏ No ❏ Yes
- ■ When mistakes happen do your co-workers and bosses bring the evidence out in the open? ❏ No ❏ Yes
- ■ Do your co-workers and bosses say that they got it wrong but that they've learnt how to prevent it happening next time? ❏ No ❏ Yes
- ■ At the end of a post mortem do people feel empowered? ❏ No ❏ Yes

- ■ If you answered 'yes' to three or more of these then you're working in an organization that's trying hard – and almost succeeding – to be blame-free.
- ■ If you got three or more no's then you're working in a blame organization.
- ■ If you got two yes's and two no's then try again, this time doing one set of answers for your boss and another set for your co-workers. One of these will give at least three yes's while the other will give you at least three no's.
- ■ If the no's are for your boss then read **Freaks – Control and Other**; **Bosses – Not So Good**.
- ■ If the no's are for your co-workers then read **Betrayal**.

If you're going to survive in a blame organization then you're going to have to learn and develop all sorts of tricks to avoid getting blamed. All of this takes time and effort. It also raises a question about whether this is the right organization for you. If it is – then great. It must be really nice to be able to look forward to spending the next few years scurrying from blame shelter to blame shelter. But if it isn't the right organization for you then it's time to prepare for a move (*see* **Résumés and Other Stories**; **To Boldly Go**).

Really good bosses are very rare animals indeed and they usually hide under a variety of guises – often to escape the wrath of their less capable or talented comrades (*see* **Bosses – Not So Good**; **Bosses – Terrible**). Because of this rarity they have great value and are often hunted by others who need their skills and abilities. The disguises under which they hide include:

- **The 'I'm not sure about this – what do you think' boss.** Underneath this facade of apparent incompetence there lurks a very competent and agile mind which sees the value of involving people and tapping into their skills, abilities and creativity.

- **The 'Let me know if you have a problem' boss.** Apparent indifference or laziness masks a willingness to trust people and allow them the space to do their own thing.

> *'I've always found that the speed of the boss is the speed of the team.'*
> Lee Iaocca

- **The 'Managing by wandering about' boss.** An illusory unwillingness to get down to the basics of the job – and keep the paperwork flowing – hides a keen awareness that the job is – and will always be – about people.

- **The 'My door is always open' boss.** An apparent unwillingness to prioritize her or his own workload disguises a strong commitment to the act of enabling people.

However good they appear to be, in the end, good bosses are only as good as their people. Your side of the bargain should be:

- be aware that you won't have him or her as a boss forever, so learn as much as you can while he or she is there
- remember that she or he is human too and can have off days or blind spots
- respond to her or his trust by managing yourself well.

The way things are these days, you're going to find yourself with a new boss sooner, rather than later. This can happen when you move or when the old boss moves on (*see* **Downsizing**; **We're Going To Have To Let You Go**; **To Boldly Go**). Whatever the cause, the situation is pretty much the same. There's a new relationship to be built, a new set of rules to be learnt (*see* **Unwritten Rules**) and a new track record to be created. But neither of you comes to this situation without a history. The grapevine (*see* **Grapevines**; **Gossip**) will have been at work. He or she will have heard about the best (and worst) of your track record and you will have been told about how he or she expects people to work until eight every evening as well as taking work home at the weekend. Of course, the accuracy of this isn't all it might be. But that's not the point. For if you or your new boss let it, this grapevine gossip can start a process that will lead to suspicion, bias, and prejudice – and that's before you've started working together! Once you do start working together things should get easier – after all, the uncertainty should get less – but that doesn't always happen.

So, here are the ten rules of new boss survival:

1 Don't jump to judgement – at least wait until you've had your first success – or row – together.
2 Let the past go – don't keep going on about how your last boss did it.
3 If you don't know or aren't sure – ask.
4 Review your strengths and past achievements – and get ready to do better.
5 Recognize your weak points and past mistakes – and restart with a clean sheet.
6 Working well together doesn't happen overnight – so give it time and work at it.
7 Remember that she or he may be subject to pressures that you're not aware of and can have good days and bad days.
8 Negotiate – honestly, openly but assertively – when you hit a rough spot and be prepared to compromise.
9 Communicate, communicate and communicate.
10 Remember that it isn't mandatory to fall in love with your new boss – you don't even have to like each other – but do respect each other.

BOSSES – NOT SO GOOD

The first symptom of working for one of these is that you don't like getting up in the morning to come to work. Some mornings you don't – hence the high figures for sickness absence. A bad boss will interpret this in a variety of ways – all of which assume that it's your problem, rather than a shared one. The truth is more likely to be that you don't like coming to work because she or he:

- doesn't give you the space to make your own decisions, or
- needs to control everyone either by coercion (threats, bullying) or manipulation (lying, politics and deceit) because he or she is scared that it will all get out of control – and he or she will lose his or her job, or
- isn't up to the job.

But the fact remains that all managers, even the bad managers, are human beings – which means that they act in whatever way they do because it gives them what they want or need. But does it? Actually, it's more likely that the way they behave really only reinforces a particular view of the world that they learnt elsewhere and earlier. To put it another way, they manage the way that they do in order to gain the certainty of knowing that the world really is the way that they think it is. While all this is nice and safe for them, it leaves us with our needs unanswered and the necessity of living in the gap between our not-so-good boss's 'world' and the real one. All of this is not good – either for us or for the organization – and you need to get out of that gap as quickly as you can.

This can be done in a variety of ways:

1 **Underground activity.** This involves undermining the boss so that he or she is moved elsewhere or sacked. While you may feel like doing this it's *not* an advisable strategy. It's *very* high risk – the tables can easily be turned on you, leading to you getting the sack. Even if it succeeds you might find that the new boss is just as bad or even worse.

2 **Viewing the high ground.** Take a look around you at the managers in other departments at the same or higher level than your boss – are they the same as her or him? If they aren't then pick the one that you know or like and approach them – in confidence and for

help (*see* **Trust; Betrayal**). If they are the same as your boss then you may have to face a difficult fact – that the culture of the organization is not one that you are compatible with (*see* **Archaeology – Corporate**).

3 **Become a covert agent for change.** This is much more fun and involves you in joining that band of unsung heroes to whom this book is dedicated and who are trying to change their organizations from the inside (*see* **Change**).

4 **Find somewhere else that has better bosses.** This is your ultimate sanction and should only be undertaken after you've tried all of the above (*see* **To Boldly Go**).

To get your boss to change you have to build a bridge across the gap between the real world and his or her world. This means that you need to do things like:

■ offering him or her solutions rather than problems;

■ making suggestions about doing it better – which he or she can pick up, use and get credit for;

■ stressing the team spirit that exists (even if it doesn't yet) and that he or she could tap into and join.

This is not a job for the overly ambitious or the fragile amongst us – it takes time, a skin like a rhinoceros and the patience of a saint – but it does produce results and you might even get to like your boss.

'So . . . tell me what you think of my ideas.'

Fortunately, *really* bad or terrible bosses are rare – even rarer than good bosses (*see* **Bosses – Good**) – but when they do occur their behaviour goes beyond mere incompetence. They can be and almost always are destructive, manipulative, untruthful, excessively egocentric and very, very selfish. Working for managers who behave in these ways – which can be described as sociopathic – constitutes a lesson on how *not* to manage. But it's also an experience which may put at risk your survival and damage your future ability to manage well. Realizing that you're working for one of these bosses is not an instant, sudden, 'Road to Damascus' experience. All the warning signs will have been there early in your relationship but you'll have chosen to ignore them. This will have been due to the fact that you couldn't believe that someone could be *that* bad and still hold down that job. Even when the mist of self deception has lifted you will have stayed – in order to make it work – somehow. But, very bad bosses *are* that bad and they *do* hold down that sort of post – because they lie to, mislead and manipulate not only the people who work for them but also their own bosses.

These sorts of boss are great survivors – but at enormous cost to those who work for them. So if your intuition starts giving you messages about a potential boss, then you should listen to it and start to check with the people who work for him or her. If you ignore or override these messages and find yourself actually working for a terrible boss – then what you need is an effective damage limitation system that protects you until you can get out (*see* **To Boldly Go**). That 'getting out' must become a priority in order to limit the damage to you. You must recognize that you *cannot* win with a genuinely terrible boss so getting out is not only sensible, it's also logical. Leaving them to sit, like spiders, in the centre of their webs of deceit and abuse will aid others to recognize and hence avoid them. It will also lead to their self-destruction as their behaviour becomes more and more extreme – as it inevitably will.

Bull, according to the *Oxford English Dictionary*, is talk or writing which is 'trivial, insincere or untruthful'. People who use it are said to bluff their way through or out of difficult situations by 'talking emptily or boastfully'. Bull, and its close cousin bull ——, are, like the common cold, almost endemic to our organizations. In some of these they have become so deeply ingrained (*see* **Archaeology – Corporate**) that the managers of these organizations have lost the ability to discriminate between what is, and what isn't, bull. When this happens the symptoms – like increasing staff turnover or losing good customers – are clear to see but usually ignored. This is because the managers have lost the ability to see or tell the truth and then, finally and fatally, begin to believe their own lies. However, this extreme addiction to bull is relatively rare and, in most organizations, bull is generally recognized for what often it is – a knee jerk and panic reaction to the sudden and awful awareness that you don't know as much as you thought you did.

Overcoming that experience, without using bull, requires the ability to say 'I don't know'. This ability is rare. It's also one that demands real skill, courage and honesty. But, since we are all members of the human race (yes, even the **Bosses – Terrible**) we often succumb to temptation and try to bull our way out of situations. But bull avoidance isn't just desirable, it's also really quite simple. Getting it right is good for your survival rating and involves the following steps:

1   Only open your mouth when you know what you're talking about.
2   If you don't know the answer but feel that you have to say something, then say: 'I don't know – but I'll find out.'
3   If you forget both the above and panic overcomes you, remember that there are two quite different sorts of bull:
     –   **Type A** – which bores and embarrasses the listener, and
     –   **Type B** – which entertains the listener but which, on detection, reverts to Type A bull *unless* you finish with the magic words: 'I don't know – but I'll find out.'

BULLYING

Bullying is out of the classroom and the playground – it's now entered the workplace. It's also changed. Workplace bullying isn't limited to the acts of physical aggression that we met in our schooldays (*see* **Aggression**). Now it comes at us in all forms and from all directions. It can happen when your boss rejects – without good reason – your proposed leave dates or when she or he – also without good reason – won't agree to your request for off-the-job training. It happens when you're given a task that you – because you haven't been trained – have no chance of successfully completing. It's there when the people you work with gossip maliciously or use bad or abusive language when they know that you don't like it. In these and many, many, other ways bullying makes its presence felt in organizations. Indeed, it's so common that it's probably been there all the time – we've just got better at recognizing it.

But why does bullying happen? The causes of bullying in the workplace are by no means straightforward or obvious. They're also as diverse as the ways in which it makes its presence felt. For example, people will bully you – or at least try to – because they think that you've more friends than they have, because you perform better at work than they do or because you got a raise and they didn't. They'll also bully you – or try to – because you're smaller than they are, younger or older than they are (*see* **Ageism**) or because you speak with a different accent to theirs or because your ethnic background is different to theirs (*see* **Racism**). Whatever the reason for the bullying, its results are the same. Being subject to prolonged bullying is a stressful experience (*see* **Winding Up and Winding Down**). Stress – or rather, too much stress – can lead to depression, anxiety or panic attacks, that not-wanting-to-get-out-of-bed-to-come-to-work feeling and ultimately, sickness absence or even that 'we're-going-to-have-to-let-you-go' situation (*see* **We're Going To Have To Let You Go**). All of this is wasteful, inefficient and unnecessary.

So how can you stop this happening to you? Here are some ideas that have stood the test of time and the bullying workplace:

- Check out your job description – be clear about what is your job.
- Keep a record of bullying incidents – dates, times, details, witnesses and how you felt.

- Confront the bully – tell them quietly, politely but assertively (*see* **Assertion**) that you take issue with their behaviour.
- If you can't manage doing that on your own, check (quietly and discreetly) with other people in your workplace. You may find that others are suffering too and that you've more support than you thought. If that's so, then see the bully together and make a collective complaint.
- Try to reduce the level of bullying by not being alone with the bully.
- Start working on yourself. Raise your self-esteem, learn how to manage your stress and get some training in being constructively assertive.
- Find out if your employer has a policy on bullying or guidelines on what sort of behaviour is – and isn't – acceptable in the workplace.
- If none of this works then take the evidence that you've gathered to an independent third party – one who has some sort of power or authority. They may be in your labour union or the equal opportunities manager, welfare officer, health and safety or personnel officer of your organization. Make sure that the formal complaint that you make to them is objective, factual and untainted by any suggestion of ambition or malice on your part.
- Remember, *nobody* has the right to bully or intimidate you.

'Well I think we ought to do that . . . and I'm bigger than you.'

BUZZWORDS

Buzzwords are fashionable 'in' words. They often have their origins in the technical vocabularies of specialists (*see* **Jargon**) and are usually used to impress rather than inform. But buzzwords can also be created or synthesized to meet a need – as in 're-engineer' or 'downsize' – and can also be words that are not in common usage or are obscure in meaning, as in 'subsume' or 'peripatetic'. Buzzwords often clump together in groups – called buzz-phrases. Careful and skilful use of a buzz-phrase can have the effect of stunning the reader or listener as his or her attention spirals off into ever-decreasing feedback loops – usually focused around a phrase like 'What on earth did that mean?' The resulting fugue-like state can last for some seconds and is often exploited by the speaker to slip in a contentious or provocative statement such as 'You're sacked' or 'We can't meet the delivery date', in the hope that this will not gain the full attention of the listener.

Some people seem to have in-built buzzword generators – they generate them with apparent ease, spinning them off quickly and apparently spontaneously. But for the rest of us the question is not so much '*how* to generate buzzwords?' but '*why* should we generate buzzwords?' Buzzwords don't increase the depth of our conversations (*see* **Conversations**), nor do they add to the quality of our communications (*see* **Communication**). But, given the ways of the work-a-day world, buzzwords look like being around for a while. So, for the rest of us, here is a simple buzz-phrase generator. Take a word from column 1, add to it a word from column 2 and then add a word from column 3 – as in 'overall binary mobility' or 'optimized synchronous software'. Try building your own version – but use it with care!

Buzz-phrase Generator

Column 1	Column 2	Column 3
Overall	Paradigmatic	Formulation
Systematic	Correlative	Projection
Conceptualized	Binary	Software
Optimized	Synchronous	Capacity
Operational	Logistic	Parameters
Integrated	Managerial	Programmes
Synergistic	Peripatetic	Mobility

CALL YOURSELF UP

The best way of finding out what you sound like to your customers (*see* **Customers**) is to call yourself up. A good time to do this is when you're away on a business trip. But don't use your special number – go through the switchboard instead. After all, that's what the customer does. See how many rings it takes before you get an answer and check out the quality of that answer. If you're lucky it'll be a person that answers, so try to focus on how friendly and welcoming they sound. If you get locked into one of those computer-driven answering systems it's very important that you check out the tone and understandability of the announcements that you get shunted through. The first time you do this you'll probably be horrified. It'll make you wonder how any of your customers manage to get through to you or how they have the patience and perseverance to survive the maze of your organization's voice mail system.

When you've got your bit of the system sorted out suggest that other people try the same thing. That way you'll all contribute to a communication system that helps you to delight your customers – rather than turns them off.

HOW NOT TO No. 1: THE INTERVIEW

Interviewer (multinational corporation department head who wants to recruit 'brighter and better staff'): *Well, that's fine. Is there anything you'd like to ask us?*

Interviewee (a young man, exceptional track record of achievement at work, wife about to produce their first child): *Yes. First, if I joined you how many hours a week would I be expected to work?; Second, if my wife has another child, do I get paternity leave and third, if my child gets ill and my wife is working can I take time off to take the child to the doctor?*

Interviewer: *If you're asking these questions, that means you don't want to join us. When people join us they're part of a team but we can't have people going off and doing what they want.*

Result: The interviewee turned down an offer that gave him 15% increase in salary and bonuses because he didn't like their 'style'.

CARING

The words 'organization' and 'caring' are rarely seen together. When they are, it's usually something to do with the 'caring professions', such as nurses or social workers. But are most organizations as uncaring as that, or is there something missing here? To get to an answer you have to look at what is meant by the act of caring. The *Oxford English Dictionary* provides at least five meanings for the verb 'to care'. These range from 'to sorrow or grieve' through to 'feeling concern'. If you asked the average person on the street about caring he or she would probably tell you that when you care about somebody you feel concern for them, you trouble yourself about them, you might even provide for or look after them. It is, you'll be told, what your parents did for you when you were a child. It's also what you do for your partner and your children. Caring for and being cared for are common experiences. Caring is also essential to your survival, growth and development – both inside and outside your organization.

In your organization caring is like the salt that you use in your kitchen. Just as your body needs that salt in order to be healthy, so you need caring in order to maintain and encourage healthy relationships with others. Just as your food needs salt to add to its taste, so do your relationships with others need caring to add to their variety and flavour. But too much salt can, as you know, spoil the best cooked of dishes. It can even, your doctor will tell you, put your health at risk. Similarly, too much caring stifles the healthy conflict that your organization needs; it suffocates your need to develop, explore and make mistakes. Just as too little salt leaves your food uninteresting, too little caring will lead you to 'raise your shields'. But what is the right amount of caring? If you ask any good cook (or manager) he or she will tell you that it's all down to judgement and experience. Good managers, like good cooks, know how and when to add that pinch of caring that turns disaster into triumph (*see* **Who Cares?**).

CHANGE

Change is the door the future uses to enter your life. There is nothing – except perhaps birth and death – that is as ubiquitous as change. It's around us, all of the time. It's so woven into the fabric of our lives that we almost ignore it – until, that is, it grabs our attention again! Change can be large – as when we change our houses, jobs or partners, or small – as when we wear jeans to work instead of a suit (*see* **Dressing up and Dressing Down**). We can chose or create change (*see* **Planning**) or it can enter our lives in ways that give us no choice about its when, what or how (*see* **Downsizing; We're Going To Have To Let You Go**). Change wears a considerable range of hats. It can be short-lived, one-off, recurrent, periodic, temporary, permanent or irreversible.

Most of us don't like change – or rather, to be more precise, we don't like being changed. When change threatens, we 'freeze-up', become rigid, fight against it – despite its merits and benefits. We do this because we:

■ fear the loss of something that we value, or
■ don't understood the change and its implications, or
■ don't think that the change makes sense, or
■ aren't able to cope with either the level or pace of the change.

All of these reactions may slow change down, even divert it, but they don't stop it happening. So how can you overcome your resistance to change and how can you use change itself to increase your survival rating?

The first part of the answer lies in your experience. After all, you've experienced, at one level or another, change all your life – and have survived to tell the tale. There will have been circumstances where you've accepted change willingly and with enthusiasm, particularly when you believed that what is to come is more attractive and interesting than what you have. Put simply, you've embraced change when you saw it as being to your advantage and you've rejected change when you saw it contained no advantage for you. It's this comparison between where you are and where you want to be that gives us some clues on how to overcome your resistance to change and how to use that change to increase your survival rating.

For you can guide, control and even manage your change. To do this you have to recognize that the ways in which organizations, and people, behave is a balancing act. What's being balanced are the forces which act upon us. There are a number of these forces – some of which will seek to promote a change in our behaviour and others will seek to restrain or limit that change. This balancing act or equilibrium isn't fixed or frozen – it's dynamic and interacts with the world in which you work or play. If you want to change the balance – and create a change – then you must either weaken one or all of the restraining forces, or strengthen one or all of the forces that promote change.

'The only completely consistent people are dead.'
Aldous Huxley

35

The resulting imbalance will mean that a shift or change occurs and a new balance is established. The forces can be anything which acts upon or is relevant to the situation. Guiding and managing a change to that equilibrium has the following steps:

1 Identify the situation and the forces involved.
2 Identify the goal.
3 Decide: (a) What you are going to do; and (b) When you are going to do it.
4 Do it!

To put it another way, what you do is the A–B–C of change management:

A Unfreezing from current position
B Moving to new position
C Re-freezing in new position.

Getting this right – managing change well – is a skill that can make a major contribution to your survival in your organization. It's also a transferable skill – you can carry it with you wherever you go. You can use it at work, at home and at play, and you can use it to create, control and manage change. It gives you an effective, efficient and adaptable surfboard on which you can surf the waves of change (*see* **Efficiency and Effectiveness**; **Adaptability**).

Let's start with the obvious. Communication – or rather, whether you get your communication right or wrong – is a core issue in the whole of your life. Without effective communication you would, literally and figuratively, be lost. It's just the same in your organization. It doesn't make any difference what your job is; if you're going to do it well you need to be able to communicate effectively. If you're going to survive and go on to growth and development – then the ability to communicate effectively is *the* 'must have' skill.

But time after time, studies of people who work in organizations tell us that the one thing that they complain most about is poor communication. It's either absent in any real sense or when it does occur it's poor quality stuff. There's a common, almost universal, cry – 'They don't listen to us!' The reasons for this begin to emerge when you ask managers about their communication. 'Communication? Of course I communicate with my people', they answer – 'I tell them what to do.' This view of communication is common. It's seen as a one-sided give-and-take process – you give an instruction and you take no argument. But is this real communication?

The answer, of course, is that it isn't. Real communication is a two-way process; it involves sending *and* receiving, talking *and* listening, writing *and* reading. It's no accident that you are born with two ears and only one mouth. When you communicate well you use all of these and the rest of your body. For you speak, listen, write, gesture, cry, smile, shout, whisper, frown, point and wave. The need to do all of this and to do it well isn't going to diminish in the twenty-first century. Organizations are getting flatter with fewer levels and wider spans of responsibility. More of your co-workers will be short-term or contract employees with limited loyalty to the 'company'. More of you will be working in your homes rather than in city centre office blocks. All of this means that you need to be able to communicate effectively. The first thing to recognize is that making that change – from being an *in*effective to an effective communicator – doesn't happen overnight. Being an ordinary 'hit-or-miss' communicator is easy; becoming an effective focused communicator – one who communicates consciously and hits his or her 'target' every time – takes patience, time and effort. But it's not impossible.

To do this – to get your communication right – you've got to:

- think it through and plan it;
- consciously choose its content, style and method with both care and due regard for the person you're communicating with;
- be clear about what your aims are;
- anticipate and eliminate what might cause it to fail.

Take a look at the other sections that give more detail on specific aspects of communication. Check out the written word (*see* **Write Words**), the spoken word (*see* **Yakkity-Yak**; **Conversations**; **Monologues and Chats**; **Dialogues and Discussions**) and listening (*see* **Listening**).

'Are you receiving me?'

COMPASSION

The word 'compassion' isn't one that you often find in organizations. Most of the time it's words with quite an opposite meaning, such as 'ruthless', ' exploitation' or 'pressured'. But isn't there some way that compassion can be used or applied to make your organization a better, happier place to work in?

The answer to this question begins by deciding what you really mean by compassion. For most of you, the act of compassion is one that has its roots in your emotions. You experience it when you feel anger or sorrow over the injustices or the pain that others suffer and feel moved to do something about these. The dictionary confirms this when it tells us that compassion involves 'suffering together with another, participation in suffering; fellow-feeling, sympathy'. But compassion isn't exclusively about your feelings. It can also be to do with your perceptions and understanding. When you use these to see your co-workers you can gain a sense of what has been described as 'increased connectedness'.

This sense of 'increased connectedness'will point you in the direction of a broader, more holistic, view of your organization. Through this you'll see the forces that act upon us *all*. This is quite different from the usual way that you look at your organization – one that's usually based on comparison and judgement. You might then be able to see that your old habits of comparison and competition – with their allocations of fault, guilt and blame – are part of a judgement process, one in which it is almost impossible to see where judgement ends and blame begins (*see* **Blame**). This 'increased connectedness' or compassion can lead to acceptance of others and that acceptance can lead to co-operation with them – and that might just be a good place to get to. What all this tells us is that compassion isn't something just for holy joe's or saints. It can be, if you choose it to be, an everyday experience for you. It can also be one that can, by virtue of its 'increased connectedness', lead you to work with others in ways which are more effective, make better use of your combined knowledge and are more fun.

Why not give it a try?

COMPETITION

Competition isn't just a twenty-first century phenomenon – it's been around for a long time. Because of this organizations often make the mistake of assuming that we all need to compete with each other, all of the time. Bonus systems are geared up so that the winner 'takes all' and promotions are granted on the basis of individual rather than team performance (*see* **Teams**).

But nothing could be further from the truth. When you look at humankind's history you'll soon find that our survival was based on the blending together of small, family-based, hunter-gather groups into larger and more socially complex 'tribes'. When you work together in these 'tribes' or organizations you tap into and share a larger pool of skills and knowledge. You do things that you can't do on your own. Competition – especially the 'winner-takes-all' sort – undermines, even destroys, that sharing. It incites you to pursue your own ends and ambitions, often at the expense of others. It's a win–lose way of doing things, one that destroys trust, limits co-operation and turns an organization into a jungle in which mistakes are seen as failures and blame and divide-and-rule dominate.

So what's the alternative? When you look at organizations that have become successful and remained that way what you see isn't built on the cult of ambition. It's collaboration, openness, seeing mistakes as opportunities to learn and the pursuit of excellence that count here. These are the organizations that realize that success will only come from the whole-hearted involvement of *all* the people who make up those organizations. They encourage these people to probe, explore, debate and, above all, challenge the 'what', 'where', 'why' and 'how' of their organizations – even the sacred cows of yesteryear! (*see* **Archaeology – Corporate**). There's an understanding that the ultimate judge in this competition is the customer – and he or she deserves to be delighted (*see* **Customers**). Achieving that means tapping into and harnessing the commitment and creativity of everybody in the organization. Doing that provides a 'win' for everybody – customers, managers, CEOs, employees, shareholders (*see* **Stakeholders**). It also results in organizations that are healthier and pleasanter to work in.

| # COMPROMISE

When what you want collides with what others want, you get conflict (*see* **Nose to Nose**). Organizations are full of conflicts. They occur when you compete with others to get what you want (*see* **Competition**), when you decide that you know better than someone else or when you just don't like each other. Some of these conflicts flare up like summer forest fires and then die down just as quickly, while others simmer away beneath the surface for days, weeks, even years. When this surfaces what you often get is confrontation. Confrontation involves face-to-face debate and this often leads to a stalemate, a 'Mexican' stand-off. When this happens those involved – co-workers, other managers, suppliers, customers, employees or trade unions – won't or can't back down. If you're going to resolve this situation then you're going to have to come up with answers to questions like 'Do you want to solve this stalemate?' or 'Do you want to win – at any cost?' The answers you get may tell you, for example, that you aren't prepared to back down, that you must win whatever the cost, or that you're prepared to give in because you think that you can't win. But between these extremes there lies a middle road, that of compromise.

Compromise is about deals and trade-offs, it resolves the conflicts created by incompatible goals and generates appropriate solutions when time's short. It's about results rather than who wins or who loses. You find your way to compromise by negotiating rather than by bullying, harassing or dominating (*see* **Bullying**; **Harassment**; **Dominance**) and you generate outcomes that are acceptable to everyone involved. When this happens, both sides win. If you're going to get to compromise then your negotiations (*see* **Negotiating**) will need to:

■ involve face-to-face contact;
■ use bargaining or bartering, so you can exchange things;
■ be about the future rather than the past or present;
■ be based on thorough and painstaking preparation;
■ generate mutually acceptable decisions.

Why not give it a go?

CONSENSUS

The word 'consensus' is a popular one. We read or hear almost everyday about 'consensus politics', a 'consensus of opinion' or that a 'consensus has been arrived at'. All of these phrases imply that a consensus exists when most of us have the same opinion about something. The *Oxford English Dictionary* definition of a consensus is a 'general agreement' or the 'collective, unanimous, opinion of a number of people'. In your organization, 'consensus' will rarely be used in any other than the sense of a general agreement, reflecting the fact that the odds on any average group of employees reaching a collective, unanimous, opinion must be about the same as the odds of winning the top prize in the Lottery!

So is 'consensus' one of those buzzwords (*see* **Buzzwords**) that flit in and out of fashion? You might, for example, claim that a consensus exists on a particular issue after you've talked to some of the people involved with it. How many and which people you talk to depends on things like how much time you had or how accessible these people were. All of which is perfectly reasonable, given the pressures of modern business. But the result isn't a consensus – it's really a straw-poll and can't even be said to be based on a representative sample of people. 'Consensus' slips further down the slippery slope of misuse when you only talk to those people that you see as 'low risk' people – that is people who agree with your viewpoint. The ultimate endpoint of this slide into misuse can be seen in the manager who talks to the man who sells newspapers on the street corner, and then claims to be in touch with what the 'rank and file' feel about the issue in question. Such a claim is not only false, it's also dishonest.

So then what should you do in your search for 'consensus'? One idealistic answer is that *everyone* in the organization should have the chance to take part in discussions about major policy decisions. Other, more practical and workable, answers rely on elected representatives but also give each and every employee a vote on key issues. In the end, the way that you find your consensus is up to you. One way of finding out is to ask your co-workers how they would like to do it – after all, communication is a two-way process. Be assured that if you don't ask them they'll find their own ways of telling you. Until then, don't be so arrogant as to claim that you have a consensus.

Conversations are very common events. They take place everywhere and involve anybody. Those who study these things tell us that a typical conversation involves three or four people, people who stand or sit quite close to each other. One reason for this physical closeness is obvious: the further away you stand from each other the more difficulty you have in hearing what is said. But another – and just as important – reason is that when you stand or sit as close as this you enter each other's 'personal space'. Usually, you only do this with people that you trust. But are your conversations about trust and sharing or are they about more pragmatic things such as passing the time of day, gossiping, or telling each other things? The answer is, of course, that most of the time your conversations are limited events. You enter them with preordained and limited targets, and, generally, that's all that you achieve.

But the conversation has the potential to be much more than that. It can be a very real exchange of ideas, a meeting of not only minds but also hearts; a space in which you discover your common humanity. Some of you may argue that work is not the place to have that sort of conversation. After all, you might say, you come to work to make money or generate profit – not to bare your soul. But work is also the space in which most of you use your creativity; it's where you have your great ideas or solve your major problems. Good conversations can help you to do that.

> *'Isn't it strange that we talk least about the things we think about the most.'*
> Charles A. Lindbergh

Here are some guidelines to good conversation:

- In good conversations you share your plans for the future, your regrets about the past and your anxieties about the present.
- Good conversations are where you use words to build relationships, dispel tensions and resolve conflicts.
- Good conversations aren't safe; they're risky ventures that have the potential to take you to places and ideas that you'd never dreamed of.
- Good conversations can involve you in:
    - exchanging information – talking about ideas, facts or figures
    - telling people about how you feel – 'feeling' talking

- exploring – talking for talking's sake, or 'play' talking
- social grooming – talking about stuff that helps your social 'togetherness'.

■ Good conversations contain:
- 'up-front' messages – in the information exchanged and the words used, and
- underlying 'meta-messages' – that are about relationships, attitudes, feelings etc. and are contained in how you speak those words.

■ In good conversations you behave in ways that tell others:
- what sort of a person you are
- whether you are interested in them and what they have to say,
- whether you trust them enough to share your feelings with them.

Remember that not all of your talking will take place in good conversations (*see* **Monologues and Chats**; **Dialogues and Discussions**). But it's important that you have enough good conversations to help you not only to increase your survival rating but also to change, develop and grow.

'My boss says I'm losing control. What do you think?'

Courage is a rare and special gift. But it's also one that you can never be quite sure of. You never know if you're going to have enough courage until the time comes to use it and you're never sure that you'll have it the next time you need it. It shows itself when you face danger without fear or shrinking. You can pluck it up, lose it, create the Dutch version by drinking alcohol, and have what's called 'the courage of your convictions or opinions'. Courage is often shown in singular acts of heroism as when firemen and women enter blazing buildings to rescue people. But these aren't the only ways that courage shows itself. You show courage when you stand up to do your presentation, when you say that you disagree with your boss and when, as a single parent, you go to work having left your unhappy child at the nursery or crèche. This sort of courage – the sort that appears in the small acts of your working days – is just as valid and just as significant as the sort of courage that we give medals for. It's the sort of courage that happens every day and it's the sort of courage that you need to help you to survive your organization. But it's rarely acknowledged and often overlooked.

Yet organizations are full of this sort of courage. It's the sort of courage that raises it's colours when you come to work to face yet another day under that terrible boss (*see* **Bosses – Not So Good**; **Bosses – Terrible**) or when you face racial abuse (*see* **Racism**) or harassment from the people you work with (*see* **Harassment**). So if you're one of the courageous many of our organizations – the ones who struggle to do a good job despite all these and the many other things that conspire to stop them – then award *yourself* a medal. You deserve it! But if you have difficulty finding your courage here are some things that might help:

■ Recognize that being courageous doesn't mean being free from fear.

■ Face your fear – and then put it aside.

■ Be prepared – to risk the known for the unknown.

CUSTOMERS

Organizations exist to serve customers. But this 'customer service' bit often gets forgotten or overlooked in the hurly-burly of life in the organization. Even when that doesn't happen the customer still remains remote – he or she is out there, outside the organization, at the end of a long line of other people. As a result most of you don't really know who your customers are and, more importantly, what they want or need. Some of you might not even care! Yet most of you would subscribe to the view that the customer *is* important – in some way or another. The reason for all this starts to become clearer when you realize that your experience of 'the customer' is, primarily, that of being one. As a customer, people serve you in shops or sell you a newspaper at the corner stand. These relationships are direct and often face-to-face. You aren't a remote and distant voice on the 'phone or a signature on a letter. But with even the best of your organization's quality training materials (*see* **Training**) the customer is an abstract entity, distant, cold and remote. Most of you will have difficulty in reconciling these two sorts of customer. As a result you'll probably cling to the abstract idea of the customer. After all, abstract entities can be dealt with – rather than related to – and you don't have to be considerate or listen to an abstract entity. At its worst, the resulting version of 'Customer Care' leaves real customers feeling that they have been processed rather than responded or listened to. At its best it is a poor substitute for the interplay and dynamics of a real relationship, however transitory that might be.

If you want to increase your survival rating then you'll need to do something about this. Start by looking at the internal customer relationships that exist within your work team. Ask yourself whether these are utility relationships – as in useful, advantageous, or profitable – or value-added relationships in which the value of the relationship increases at each transaction. True customer relationships – internal and external – are based on value.

You're all, whether you like it or not, in the choice business. You choose what to have for dinner, whether to have a shower or a bath, whether to marry this person or that one and, sometimes, whether or not to make war. When you do that you make a decision. Sometimes you make a 'bad' decision and find yourself at a 'wrong' endpoint and other times you make a 'good' decision and arrive at the 'right' endpoint. The time that you spend in your workplace is particularly rich in these decisions. You decide which of the many tasks that face you to tackle first, how you approach and undertake that task, at what time you make that important telephone call, when you break for coffee and whether you talk to the boss about that persistent problem. A lot of these workplace decisions are about minor, relatively inconsequential, things and you take them easily, almost without thinking. But some of them are big decisions – involving high levels of risk or with consequences that are expensive. Most of you aren't very good at taking these big decisions – you worry about them, you grapple with them, they steal your sleep. Part of the reason for this lies in the way that you've learnt to take your decisions. For most of you learnt, initially, by watching your parents take decisions and then by doing it yourself – by experience, by trial and error. This sort of learning brings with it some bad decision-taking habits, as well as some good ones. The other reason why you're often not good at taking 'big' decisions lies in the fact that when you face them, you:

■ haven't taken many of this sort of decision before, and
■ haven't got a lot of information about:
  – the choices you face
  – the facts and figures associated with those choices, and
  – the risks involved.

The combination of lack of experience and lack of information can be pretty lethal. It's a combination that can keep you awake at night as well as raising your blood pressure when you worry about your lack of answers to questions like 'what if…?' But, this can be overcome; you can learn to throw off your bad decision-taking habits from the past. Doing this can upgrade your ability to survive in your organization. So here are some steps towards doing just that:

■ Make sure that you've defined the problem correctly.
■ Make sure that you know what your choices are.
■ Check out whether you've got enough information.
■ If the answer's 'no, you haven't', then either:
  – postpone the decision until you have that information, or
  – spend time and money getting that information.
■ If the answer's still 'no' and you can't delay your decision any longer then make it using these rules:
  1 Take the choice that will leave everyone at least as well off as they were before it and makes at least one person better off (Pareto's Principle), or
  2 Take the choice that minimizes the maximum loss (Minimax loss), or
  3 Find a 'good enough' decision based on the information that you've got by looking at each alternative in turn until you find one that's good enough – and then stop looking (Satisficing).
■ If you know what your choices are or what the problem is *and* you've enough of the right sort of information then:
  – identify the outcome that you want;
  – compare each choice's predicted outcome to your desired outcome;
  – choose the one that's nearest.
■ Monitor how well the outcome of your decision works – so that you can make a better or quicker decision next time.

HOW NOT TO No. 2: PEOPLE CARE

The manager of a telephone line insurance company gave each of his staff a packet of tissues and a fun-size chocolate bar – after he'd told them they were all being made redundant.

There's a lot of delegation about these days. Some of this is happening because your organizations are smaller and flatter then they used to be (*see* **Downsizing**; **Organizations**) and some of it is happening because your managers are too busy (*see* **Times a'wasting**) or aren't as good as they used to be (see **Bosses – Not So Good**; **Bosses – Terrible**). There's also a problem with the quality of that delegation. For, hidden under it's cloak, you'll also find the acts of dumping, down-loading and passing the buck. But *real* delegation is different from all of these. A manager or supervisor who really delegates – rather than dumps or off-loads – is one who takes risks with his or her co-workers. He or she entrusts huge chunks of his or her authority to them – not out of laziness or irresponsibility but in order to create a climate in which they can learn (*see* **Training**) and hence grow. This learning–growing sequence lies at the heart of real delegation. Without it, the delegation becomes a sham; the act of a manager who is, at best, confused and, at worst, duplicitous. Here are some check points to help you sort out real delegation from the not-so-real:

> 'And Moses chose able men out of all Israel, and made them heads over the people, rulers of thousands, rulers of hundreds, rulers of fifties, and rulers of tens. And they judged the people at all seasons: the hard cases they brought unto Moses, but every small matter they judged themselves
>
> Exodus 18:25–26

- A *real* delegating manager has sorted out the when, what, how and why of the task *before* he or she talks to you.
- You'll *really* get delegated to when you've got the skills needed – rather than just because you've got some time available or because you won't say 'no' (*see* **Assertion**).
- When the task is passed to you a *real* delegating manager will:
  - explain the what, how, why and when of it;
  - give you the chance to ask for any training, equipment or facilities that you'll need;
  - ask you if you're willing to accept the task;
  - give you the credit for a job well done.

DIALOGUES AND DISCUSSIONS

Some of your conversations (*see* **Conversations**) will make a difference to your working days. In these you'll really interact with others; your understanding of them or the subject you're discussing will be upgraded. These are the conversations that you remember. They will not only make a difference to your working day, they'll also upgrade your survival rating.

What goes on in these conversations can be described as a dialogue or a discussion. The differences between these are subtle but important. The dialogue, for example, appears on the surface to be an ordinary conversation between two or more persons. But it isn't. For what goes on in a true dialogue is quite different. In the true dialogue, you leave your roles, positions, prejudices and preconceptions 'at the door'. You learn through words, your understanding is extended or enhanced. Insights are gained and perspectives are shifted – sometimes radically. These changes go well beyond what happens in an ordinary run-of-the-mill conversation and well beyond what you could gain on your own.

The discussion also takes us beyond the boundaries of ordinary conversation. It involves debate, with cases argued for and against. Its objective is to ventilate a question, to elicit truth or establish a point. During a discussion, a question or subject is treated from several different viewpoints until a conclusion or endpoint is reached. Its endpoint lies beyond that which you could have reached on your own.

Both of these have the potential to become major elements of your communications toolbox. But if you are going to learn to use them and allow them to contribute to your organizational survival and growth then you have to deliberately expose yourself to them. You have to seek out and find those in your workplace who are skilful in their use and expose yourself to their rhetoric. You also have to polish your use of them.

'Disobedience is the true foundation of liberty. The obedient must be slaves.'

Henry David Thoreau

'DISOBEDIENCE, noun. The silver lining to the cloud of servitude.'

Ambrose Bierce

'Speak the truth, but leave immediately after.'

Slovenian Proverb

'No matter how much the cats fight, there always seem to be plenty of kittens.'

Abraham Lincoln

'To gain that which is worth having, it may be necessary to lose everything else.'

Bernadette Devlin

'It follows that any commander in chief who undertakes to carry out a plan which he considers defective is at fault; he must put forward his reasons, insist on the plan being changed, and finally tender his resignation rather than be the instrument of his army's downfall.'

Napoleon

'The more people who believe in something the more apt it is to be wrong. The person who's right often has to stand alone.'

Søren Kierkegaard

'A healthy person goes "Yes", "No" and "Whoopee." An unhealthy person goes "Yes, but", "No, but" and "No whoopee".'

Eric Berne

'The test of tolerance comes when we are in the majority, the test of courage when we are in the minority.'

Ralph W. Sockman

DOMINANCE

Every time you meet someone new the same question gets asked – and answered – namely, 'who's the dominant one?'. The dominance issue appears everywhere. It's there in the playgroups of your children, the shops of your malls, the greens of your golf courses, the changing rooms of your gyms and, of course, in the workplaces of your organization. In fact, it appears everywhere that people meet. Most of the time the question remains unspoken, almost invisible. We size one another up instinctively, almost without thinking, using ways that are almost as natural to us as breathing. The answers that you get are important – they define the small (and sometimes the large) print of your daily lives. For they tell you about where you are in the social hierarchy, what your position is in the pecking order (*see* **Pecking Order**) and what your rank is.

In animal groups, it's brute force that establishes this rank. This is supported by size, appearance and aggression (*see* **Aggression**). But when we human beings size each other up we very rarely wrestle each other to the ground in an attempt to gain submission. Studies of human body language tell you that dominance is established by the way you stand, look at each other, talk and gesture. Tall people who stand up straight with their hands on their hips and talk loudly while gazing directly, staring other people down, are seen to be dominant. Small people who speak quietly and tend to look down when spoken to are seen to be subordinate. But the way that you stand and talk isn't the only thing that establishes whether you're dominant. For you can also try to establish your dominance by helping someone. 'Let me help you' followed by the helping hand is not only much more good mannered and graceful than a dominating stare, it's also more effective. But both can have the same intention – to dominate.

Given that all this dominance stuff has been around for a long, long time, it would be foolish to suggest that you try to 'buck the trend.' But do try to be more aware of the 'who's the dominant one?' question. Choose your answer with thought and care – rather than by instinct – and try to remember that someone else's attempts at domination will only 'work' if *you* let them.

The word 'downsizing' first appeared in the late 1970s. Then, it was used to describe what happened when a car manufacturer redesigned a car so that it had smaller overall dimensions, but with the same interior, boot or trunk space. Now, things are different. These days downsizing is used to describe what happens when an organization – rather than a car – gets smaller. An astonishing number of explanations have been given for this shrinking. The adoption of a new organizational 'cure-all' – such as re-engineering, flatter structures, falling sales or profits, outsourcing, the need to get 'lean', the infamous 'first-we-merge-then-we-purge' syndrome – all of these and more have been used to justify downsizing. But all of these and the many other reasons given have the same result – getting rid of people.

If your organization is showing the symptoms of an on-coming downsize or is actually about to do it then you will find yourself in one of two positions: you're either going or you're staying. Whichever happens to you, you'll be facing a tough time. Your values will be challenged, your stress levels will rise, your health may suffer, your home life may deteriorate and your morale will plummet. These things will happen because you're either face-to-face with unemployment (*see* **We're Going To Have To Let You Go**) or having to work longer hours and harder to stay in the same place with the threat of still more redundancies looming over you.

So, given that organizational downsizing has almost reached knee-jerk status, what can you do to help yourself to survive all of this? Here are some answers:

1 Throw complacency out of the window now. Just because your individual downsizing experience hasn't started yet doesn't mean that it won't.

2 Upgrade your résumé or cv. This needs to be done *now* – not just after the downsizing announcement or when it's convenient.

3 Prepare yourself for change. Start thinking about how you'd cope if the rug was pulled from under you. Work out your responses, check your options and your facts and figures, get your mind ready.

4 Be realistic. Being unrealistic about what might happen to you is just like sticking your head in the sand. Get your head into the air and look around. Acknowledge and confront the risks that you're facing.

5 Find people to talk to. Lay-offs hurt and talking about that hurt or even just your fear of it can be an enormous help. Find someone outside your workplace and your family to do this with – someone you trust. Don't expect your boss or your organization to help with this – they've got their own problems.

6 Don't use alcohol, drugs, food or other chemicals to prop youself up. Stuff like this will only make you feel better in the short term. It's better, in the long term, for you to take regular exercise, communicate more and set time aside each day to relax. If this gets to be a struggle then go and see your doctor. Do be honest with him or her about what's happening and how you feel about it – listen carefully to the advice that you're given.

7 Use your contacts. Getting that new job won't be easy, but what will help are your contacts. So get the word out, let them know that you're on the market (*see* **Networking**).

8 Get – and stay – positive. Being positive at a time like this isn't easy. There's no point in pretending that you're upbeat when you're not. But facing and acknowledging your negative feelings will help you to find the other side of the coin – the positive side of what's happening.

9 Rise to the challenge. See what's happening as a challenge – rather than a problem. Work at turning your downsizing experience around, from defeat to opportunity.

HOW NOT TO No. 3: PERSUASION
The Core Characteristics of Bad Persuasion

- Make your persuasion illogical, unclear and badly organized.
- Bore them with lots of facts and figures.
- Never use examples.
- Frighten them with the negatives.
- Leave out or forget about the 'it's been done before' evidence.
- Make sure that they know about the Penalties – as in 'if you don't do this...'

DRESSING UP AND DRESSING DOWN

The clothes that you wear in your organization are changing. The neck-tie and formal suit are out, the open-neck shirt and the sweater are in. 'Dress-down' Fridays have stretched out to become 'dress-down' weeks. Even accountancy firms are letting their staff come to work in 'business casual' clothes – rather than formal suits. In the European Union it's now a violation of your right to privacy and freedom of expression when your boss insists that you wear clothes that meet the company 'dress code'.

These dress codes or the 'this-is-what-we-want-to-see-you-wearing' rules have been around for a long time. In early New England women were forbidden to wear silk scarves unless their husbands were worth one thousand dollars or more. In medieval Germany women were made to wear a wooden collar if they 'dressed above their station'. For clothes do more for us than keep us warm or cover us up. The clothes you wear send social signals to everyone who sees you. These signals can tell them what your job is, what ball game you play, what club or group you belong to, what your religious beliefs are, what soccer or baseball club you support or what pop star you like. They can even indicate your social class and whether you do – or don't – follow the latest fashion.

> 'The apparel oft proclaims the man.'
> Shakespeare, *Hamlet*
> 1.3.70

But the departure of suits from your workplace doesn't really mean the end of dress codes. For what you wear at work doesn't only tell others what you do and what organization you do it for. It also sends messages about whether you fit in, whether you're part of the 'tribe'. Doing away with a formal dress code doesn't change this, it merely converts the rules from written to unwritten (*see* **Unwritten Rules**). For some of you this will be stressful. For the decisions you have to take now will no longer be of the 'which-suit-do-I-wear-today' variety. Now you'll have to decide whether today is a 'jeans-and-T-shirt' day or a 'shorts-and-trainers' day (*see* **Decisions**).

DUVET DAYS

A Duvet Day starts when you wake up and realize that today is one of those days when you just can't face going into work. What happens then is that you pull the duvet back over your head – and go back to sleep. These Duvet Days often masquerade under the guise of a 'I'm-really-too-ill-to-come-in', or sick, days – but they're really quite different. For on a sick day you really are too ill to come to work, while on a Duvet Day you just can't convince yourself that it's *worth* coming to work. A Duvet Day is a day when your dislike of your organization overwhelms your need to pay the house loan or make sure there's enough money in the bank to pay the bills. It's a day when you just don't have enough courage (*see* **Courage**) to go into battle again with that awful boss, a day when you just can't face any more of the stuff that goes on in your organization, a day when your tank runs dry. You'll probably tell yourself that it's temporary. You're tired, run-down, over-stressed. Tomorrow, you'll tell yourself, things will be different.

But will they – or is a Duvet Day a glimpse of the way things really are? The answer to this depends on how often your Duvet Days happen. When they're infrequent or occasional then they're probably a response to your (or your boss's) biorhythms, the weather or even the current phase of the Moon. But when they start to increase they carry a message for you. It's a message that tells you that things aren't as they ought to be – and something needs to be done about it. For your Duvet Days might increase because you're being harassed or bullied, mismanaged or abused or even being stalked by a Control Freak (*see* **Bosses – Not So Good**; **Bosses –Terrible**; **Bullying**; **Freaks – Control and Other**; **Harassment**). Duvet Days, or the temptation to take them, might even rise because you're ready to move on – to something bigger and better (*see* **Resumés and Other Stories**; **To Boldly Go**; **Your Future**). So keep an eye on your Duvet Days – both real and desired – and listen to what they're telling you. Resist the temptation to pull the duvet over your head – get up and do something about it!

You've all got e-mail. It floods into your computers every day and the more you send – the more you get back. Reading and answering your e-mail is the first thing that you do when you get to your office and the last thing you do before you leave. E-mail, together with the mobile phone, has become *the* way of communicating at the beginning of the twenty-first century.

But does it really work, does it really enable us to communicate with each other and does it do all that you want it to? Effective communication (*see* **Communication**) is a two-way process; one that, at its peak, enables us to freely and easily exchange both information and feelings. When you communicate in your workplace it's the four I's that you do: you instruct, interrogate, influence and inform. Most of this you do face-to-face. But e-mail isn't face-to-face. At best, it's at the other end of a chain that goes something like: you→computer→network→computer→other person. Nor is this message-passing as instant and real-time as our face-to-face communication is; it's buffered, displaced and desynchronized by the nature of the technology involved. But this has its advantages, for when you use your e-mail systems you're able to consider carefully what you write; to copy and keep a record of your messages and to say what you need to without having to respond to or cope with the response it generates. But these and other advantages are also present in the notes and letters of your snail mail systems. But e-mail is faster, easier, more 'instant' than snail mail. And therein lies it's downside.

Most e-mails are ill-composed and unclear with a high potential for misinterpretation or misunderstanding. But that's not the only risk you run when you use e-mail systems. For the ease of use and accessibility of the e-mail means that it provides an outlet for the frustrations of the workplace. Most of you will have received 'flame-mail' – derogatory, inappropriate even obscene e-mail messages. You can't walk away from or interrupt these – as you could if they were delivered face-to-face – and telling the sender 'where to go' in the same style can put you at risk. For when you send an e-mail its contents are as public and open as they would be if you'd chalked them on the pavement or sidewalk. Special software enables the content of your e-mail to be monitored and sometimes edited by the prohibition of specific phrases or words. The amount of time you spend sending or answering e-mail can also be monitored.

But, despite all of this, e-mail still has its gifts for you. When you use it skilfully and appropriately you can – quickly, easily and effectively (*see* **Efficiency and Effectiveness**) – keep in touch with each other. You can achieve astonishing things by using a well-timed and polished e-mail. But to do that you need to take note of the following guidelines:

- Don't use or invent a strange or even funny e-mail address – try to keep it obvious, short and easy to remember.
- Don't do your e-mail in capital letters.
- Try to find and use a font that looks good.
- Occasional typos such as 'teh' are acceptable but too many creates the impression that you're careless – or stupid.
- Get your grammar right and avoid the use of chat-room abbreviations.
- Get permission before sending personal e-mails on your work system and keep them short and to the point when you do.
- Find out if your work system is monitored.
- Don't use bad or profane language.
- Never e-mail anything that you wouldn't want your boss (or your mother) to read.
- Don't overdo it – after all, e-nough is enough.

You say that someone is eccentric when they behave in ways that are different from what is 'usual' or in ways that are 'odd' or 'whimsical'. These things are, of course, relative and what is odd or whimsical to a banker may not be so to a research chemist or to a computer programmer.

Eccentrics exist in all organizations. You all know of people who 'do their own thing' (*see* **Tall Poppies**) despite – and often in defiance of – the rules (*see* **Unwritten Rules**) and pressures of an organization. But in most organizations these eccentrics are barely tolerated – rather than accepted or nurtured – and this tolerance only continues as long as the outcomes of their eccentricity are useful to the organization. What happens when the eccentric is seen to no longer have any real or potential value is often unpleasant (*see* **We're Going To Have To Let You Go**) but, in the eyes of those who decide what is behaviourally 'right' or 'wrong' in the organization, justifiable.

All of this assumes that human behaviour can and ought to be controlled and confined to a narrow (and often arbitrary) band or spectrum. Behaviour outside that band is *not* acceptable. If you doubt the existence of this 'acceptable behaviour band' ask yourself how many workplaces that you know of in which it's acceptable to sing when you're happy or cry or shout when you're upset or angry (*see* **Singing**). The answer is very, very, few. But why is this; why can't you display your feelings at work? The answer lies in the fact that your organization needs you to behave in ways that are (a) predictable and (b) safe. But where does all this conformity get you? Does it enable you to be creative and make real and sometimes magnificent contributions to the well-being and success of your organization? Of course it doesn't – nor will it ever – and that's where eccentricity comes in. For, hand in hand with its integral nonconformity, eccentricity brings you rare and precious gifts – high levels of creativity, insatiable curiosity and the need to make the world a better place. Can you really afford to crush or even destroy these characteristics in the vice of organizational conformity? Nurture and protect your eccentricity. For with it you might just be in the advance guard of those who are the first to see the emerging organizations of your new future.

EFFICIENCY AND EFFECTIVENESS

Efficiency and effectiveness are words that are frequently used in organizations. You might tell people, for example, that you've 'got an efficient operation' or persuade them how effective the changes that you made have been. Most of the time, though, you use these words incorrectly, even interchangeably, and in ways that are remote from their original meanings. As a result they've become devalued. Linguists tell us that this blurring of original meanings is one of the ways in which a language evolves and generates new words. This may mean that, in time, you may be using new and combined versions of these words – such as 'effectency' or 'efficitiveness'. However, until that happens, it's worth revisiting their original meanings to see if they still have any value for you.

Efficiency is concerned with outcomes and inputs and is usually expressed as the ratio of work done (the outcome) to energy or effort consumed (the input). You can think of an organization as a mechanism that converts inputs – such as raw materials, information, money, etc. – into outputs such as more money, more or different information, cars, products, etc. An efficient organization requires less or fewer inputs than an inefficient organization to produce the same output. This is just the same sort of thing that happens when a car that's less efficient than another will consume more petrol for the same mileage or when an inefficient person takes more time or uses more resources – such as paper, electricity, computer time etc. – to produce the same result (or output) as an efficient person.

Effectiveness, however, is different. It's primarily concerned with the nature of the outcomes. Something that's effective generates not only the result that you want, it also produces it where and when you want it. An effective salesperson, who may or may not be efficient, is one who achieves repeat orders and satisfied customers. Doing that may mean spending a lot of time talking to customers without an immediate or apparent result. This will be seen as inefficient (in terms of sales income per unit of salesperson time) – but it is effective.

If you limit the way you monitor your work to its efficiency then you're in danger of forgetting the need to satisfy and delight the customer. But if you fling efficiency out of the window in a frenzied attempt to satisfy each and every customer need you're then in danger of either getting the sack or, if you work for your own organization, becoming bankrupt. What's needed is a balance between the two, a balance that recognizes that they are linked together and that if you ignore either of them you put the other at risk. Loosen up and try to recognize either that efficiency isn't the answer to everything or that effectiveness may not pay your bills. Try to be more aware of the need to balance your use of and commitment to these factors. Tilt a little by easing back on the efficiency pedal and taking the time to *really* find out exactly what your customers (*see* **Customers**) need as well as where and when they need it. If you think you already know this then spend a little more time seeing how you can answer those customer needs with less expenditure of time or energy.

HOW NOT TO No. 4: THE E-MAIL

The following e-mail was sent to Sharon, a senior manager in a non-profit making organization. Due to recruiting difficulties caused by a rigidly applied and inadequate salary system her department had been 40 per cent understaffed for over a year. Despite this, she and her very committed staff had managed to maintain a high level of user service. She had agreed both the timing and content of her response to the audit referred to with Elisa, her immediate manager.

✎ From the Office of the Deputy Director

To: Sharon

Cc: Elisa

I have to express my great disappointment with your response to the Audit. It is not acceptable that your response is faxed in during my meeting with Elisa. You must take the issues raised more seriously. As a learning organization we all must take self monitoring seriously. You will attend a meeting with Elisa and me in my office on Tuesday next at 3.00pm.

Mary

Deputy Director

Within six months Sharon and her key team leaders had left the organization – leaving a demoralized and even more understaffed department. As a result of the highly critical findings of the next biannual audit, Mary went through her own individual learning curve – she was sacked.

EMPATHY

Empathy is another of those words that have jumped into common use – or misuse – from specialized vocabularies of experts (*see* **Jargon**). The word first appeared some 100 years ago, being the English version of the German word 'einfühlung' or 'one-feeling'. Originally, it was associated with the study of aesthetics and meant the ability to project one's personality or feel oneself into whatever it was that was being contemplated, and so fully comprehend it. But psychologists and social scientists use empathy differently. For they use it to mean the ability to put yourself in another's shoes, to the extent that you feel what they feel. Doing this is different from feeling what you think they feel or feeling what you feel about them. It's about what they are actually feeling. Carl Rogers, one of the pioneers of humanist psychology, describes empathy as being about sensing the other's private world 'as if it were your own'. But both of these meanings are quite different from our common usage of empathy, for now it's used as a fashionable alternative to sympathy. These days you say that you have empathy towards somebody when you care for them or have positive feelings about them. But is that what empathy is really about and, if it is, what can it contribute to your survival rating?

The answer to this question begins with the fact that you'll only be able to survive and achieve success in the organizations of the twenty-first century by working through and with your co-workers (*see* **People**). What this means is that you must be able to link up with and share the creative skills and abilities of these people. A key skill in that process is that of listening (*see* **Listening**), not just to the words but also the feelings of these people. That's where empathy comes in. For when you are empathic you:

- can understand what others are feeling;
- have no doubt or uncertainty about what those feelings are;
- say things that are compatible with those feelings;
- behave in ways that fit in with those feelings.

Being empathic towards your co-workers isn't about being 'soft and cuddly', it's about treating them as equals and respecting their right to have and express feelings about what goes on in the workplace. Try it – you might even find that they respect your right to have and express feelings too!

The verb 'to empower' isn't a new one. It first appeared in the English language some time between the fifteenth and seventeenth centuries. Then it was used to describe what happened when a king (or some similar authority) formally bestowed power on somebody, usually towards a specific end or for a certain purpose. Now, in the twenty-first century, its use and meaning have expanded well beyond those regal boundaries. Empowerment has become one of those buzzwords that are used (and misused) everywhere (*see* **Buzzwords**). If you doubt this, try putting 'empowerment' into your internet search engine and see how many returns you get! If you click on these you'll find that many are about a process that's very different to the one that's described above. For now, empowerment, in its simplest form, leads to people being responsible for what they do. That responsibility can be given or it can be taken.

Giving responsibility to people is by far the most common form of empowerment. It's been fashionable for so long that it's almost old-fashioned. It should be a part of every managers' toolkit. But that doesn't mean that they all know how to use it or are willing to do so. There are still managers who are confused between the very different acts of delegation and empowerment, managers who think that empowerment happens when they tell you what they want and then leave you to get on with it and managers who think that empowerment is just another way of describing a chaotic free-for-all (*see* **Delegation**). But if not all managers have moved on, empowerment has.

For now it's become something that you can take for yourself – rather than have given to you by others. This form of empowerment is far more potent and powerful than the given version. It's also more portable – you can take it with you when you change jobs – and more demanding, asking more of you in its creation. Here are some rules to help you to achieve successful self-empowerment:

> *'Power can be taken but not given. The process of taking is empowerment in itself.'*
> Gloria Steinem

1 Decide what you want from your empowerment.

2 Create your personal self-empowerment plan.

3 Find people who can help you to do it.

4 Identify the barriers to your empowerment.

5 Prepare yourself for empowerment.

6 Make sure you've got the skills/knowledge needed.

7 Negotiate your new responsibilities, targets and objectives.

8 Take one step at a time.

9 Build on your successes.

10 Learn from your failures.

11 Review your progress every 90 days.

12 Update your self-empowerment plan.

Remember that empowerment – even in the twenty-first century – still means giving power. In this case it's self-empowerment – you giving yourself the power you need to survive, grow and develop. When you do this what you'll find is that things will change. For now you'll be able to:

■ set up and drive your own projects (*see* **Projects**);

■ solve problems – for yourself and others (*see* **Decisions**);

■ re-invent yourself – when it's needed (*see* **Re-invention**);

■ create your own future (*see* **Your Future**); and

■ find, and use, your own brand of courage (*see* **Courage**).

'If I don't enjoy myself, there's no point in turning up.'

Radio talk show presenter

'Everything has become so ghastly and corporate and false and full of faxes and high technology – there should be more room for fun!"

Paul Smith

'Things generally go wrong – so you might as well start to enjoy it.'

Anon

'When we started the business it was a lark. We used to say we'd do it for a few years and then become cross-country truck drivers.'

Jerry Greenfield of Ben & Jerry's IceCream

'This business is as much fun as you can have with your clothes on.'

John Hegarty

'Are we having fun yet?'

Carol Burnett

'If you're going to do something wrong, at least enjoy it.'

Leo Roston

'Let him who would enjoy a good future waste none of his present.'

Roger Babson

'Like what you do, if you don't like it, do something else.'

Paul Harvey

'Just play. Have fun. Enjoy the game.'

Michael Jordan

'People who enjoy what they are doing invariably do it well.'

Joe Gibbs

'If your capacity to acquire has outstripped your capacity to enjoy, you are on the way to the scrap heap.'

Glen Buck

'Enjoy the journey, enjoy every moment, and quit worrying about winning and losing.'

Matt Biondi

EXCELLENCE

These days, excellence is a much sought after, much aspired to, state of affairs. You achieve it when you make or do something that is superior, something that surpasses everything around it. You get to it when you outdo the efforts of others. But the road to excellence isn't an easy one; it demands hard work and dedication. Nor does it happen overnight; it takes time both to prepare for and to travel the road to excellence. You may have already come across some of the things that will contribute to your excellence in the other pages of this book. You may have already read about adaptability (*see* **Adaptability**), answering the needs of customers (*see* **Customers**) and effectiveness (*see* **Efficiency and Effectiveness**). You may have touched on the sections about flexibility (*see* **Flexibility**) and Total Quality Management (*see* **Quality**). If you haven't got to these yet, then make a note to do so, but after you've read this section.

But getting to excellent isn't the only struggle that you face. Once you're there you face another struggle – the struggle to stay there. For excellent isn't an absolute condition – it's a relative one. You say something is excellent when you compare it to other things, rather than by comparison to an absolute standard. This means that what is excellent now will be ordinary, what's expected, tomorrow. If you doubt this, look at the way that the specifications and fittings of cars have changed over time. Optional and costly extras are now standard features. This means that in your struggle to survive and grow in your organization, this year's excellent will become the expected baseline for next year's performance.

But what are you going to become excellent at? The way that workplaces are changing that's not an easy question to answer. Certainly the answer doesn't lie in becoming a specialist or an expert in a narrow field of knowledge. For what is special today will be either ordinary or redundant tomorrow. Nor does the answer lie at the other extreme – that of becoming a generalist, a logic-chopping systems analyst who can manipulate numbers anywhere. For it is passion and commitment that breed success, rather than cold rationality and logic. So where should your excellence lie? The answer lies in something that's obvious and easily available. For all of us, without exception, can be excellent – at being *ourselves*. The individual package of idiosyncrasies, skills, knowledge and experiences that you have is unique. Your survival rating will increase by leaps and bounds as you learn to use your special skills and abilities.

But it's better than that. For this version of excellent isn't locked into working for the XYZ Corporation or carrying out a particular role or job – it's portable, transferable excellence that goes with you wherever you go and whatever you do. But, like the sort of excellence that's specific to a role or a skill, this excellence takes time – both to prepare for and to happen. Nor is it without it's difficulties, which can be illustrated by the saying that tells us that 'the more we work on ourselves the more we seem to become like our fathers (or mothers)'. But being or becoming excellent in this way is a 'must do' in your struggle to survive in your organization. To begin, all you have to do is to let go of the idea that someone else knows (or knew) what you should do with your life. This sort of excellence is a state of mind, rather than a process or an A–B–C. What you'll find, as you move along its road, is that you've actually more experience of being excellent in this way than you thought you had when you started.

'Today filing clerk . . . tomorrow manager.'

FEEDBACK

If you go to rock concerts or have a teenager who deafens you with their attempts to play an electric guitar, you'll be no stranger to feedback. It's that loud, whistling, shrieking, dissonant, noise that happens when an electric guitar is too close to its amplifier. But if you look up the word feedback in a dictionary you'll find something different. Here feedback is 'the modification, adjustment, or control of a process or system (as a social situation or a biological mechanism) by a result or effect of the process, especially by a difference between a desired and an actual result'. There's no trace of dissonance or loudness here. It's about adjustments that follow the comparison of actual and desired performance. So which of these versions do you experience in your organization and, more importantly, which of them is going to help you survive that organization? The answer, for most of you, is that while the sort of feedback that you get at work *ought* to be closer to the dictionary version, it's actually often closer to the rock concert guitar version. So why and how does that happen?

Whatever job you do, you feel good when you're told that you're doing it well. It makes you happier and you feel motivated. But what happens when you're told the opposite, that you're not working well? The answer, of course, is that you start to feel unhappy and demotivated; you might even get angry. But what's even worse than that is the way that you feel when you sense that something isn't quite right, when – despite your best efforts – your boss seems unhappy with you but doesn't, or can't, say why. What happens then is that you become uneasy and unsure. Distrust, doubt and suspicion rear their ugly heads. In all of these situations you're getting feedback. But the sort of feedback that you've been given in each case is very different. In the last case – where your boss couldn't or wouldn't tell you what was wrong – the feedback that you got was indirect, ill-defined and ambiguous. You were left feeling that you'd done something wrong, but not sure what it was. In the first two cases – where you were told that you've done well or badly – you were given direct and unambiguous feedback.

But what you weren't given, in any of these situations, was the opportunity to use and learn from that feedback. When this happens – when you get the opportunity to learn – then your feedback switches into a constructive mode of operation. Constructive feedback is fair, accurate and clear – anything less will leave you with a feeling that you're being 'got at' or that gossip (*see* **Gossip**) is being recycled. It gives you the opportunity to find out more – how to do it even better or how to stop doing it wrong. It can also be a two-way process – a good boss (*see* **Bosses – Good**) will be willing to both give and receive feedback.

Constructive feedback can make a major contribution to your survival rating. Giving it and doing that well is a rare art. It's also a learning situation – for both the giver and the receiver. It's usually 90° feedback, as between your supervisor and you. But it can also be

> '*I do not resent criticism, even when, for the sake of emphasis, it parts for the time with reality.*'
> Winston Churchill

360° feedback and involve the views of all the people around you in your workplace, including your supervisor, your co-workers, your customers and those you supervise.

Here are some guide points towards making sure that your feedback is constructive and well done – whether it's 90° or 360°:

- Prepare your feedback – make sure you're clear about what you want to say and why.
- Be realistic about the time needed – make sure that you've both got the time needed to say all that you need to say.
- Make sure that the feedback session is private and uninterrupted.
- Not everyone is good at giving or accepting feedback, so listen carefully (*see* **Listening**) to what they do – and don't – say and adjust the pace and rhythm of what you say to suit.
- Be positive at the beginning, build trust and openness.
- Check your communication (*see* **Communication**) – is what you're saying being received *and* understood?
- Don't just focus on negatives – what you don't want to see – tell them what you *do* want to see.
- Look for solutions to which you both agree.
- Remember that you can't force change (*see* **Change**).

FLEXIBILITY

Flexibility – or doing it differently – is the new rock and roll of your workplace. When you're flexible, you're pliant, supple, you flex and bend with the stresses and strains of the workplace – without breaking or cracking. Being flexible is rather like being adaptable (*see* **Adaptability**) except that adaptability is about going that 'extra' mile for a customer and flexibility is about doing what you do for them differently. Flexible people don't get locked into fixed routines – they respond to the needs of their co-workers and the customer (*see* **Customers**). This responsiveness is important, for it enables you to do what you do efficiently and effectively (*see* **Efficiency and Effectiveness**). But that isn't the only side of flexibility. Technology and changing attitudes mean that not only can you be flexible in *what* you do, you can also be flexible in the *when*, *where* and the *how* of doing it. Take a look at these ways of being flexible:

- **Flexible hours.** If you've got children of school age who need to be taken to and from school, then flexible hours will be great for you. Breaking out of the 9 to 5 mould can remove much of the stress of rush hour travel and liberate you from the worries about 'who picks the children up'. It also allows your employer to keep your skill and experience.
- **Job-sharing.** Job sharing enables you to put in the hours that fit with your lifestyle and reduces the worries about the piles of work waiting for you back in the office. Like flexible hours, job sharing also gives your employer a way of keeping your skill and experience and still answering the customer's needs.
- **Teleworking.** Computer and telecommunications technology have given you the means to work at home and still keep in touch with your boss and your co-workers. This can help when you've got heavy domestic responsibilities, such as several children of school age or under, or when you're a carer for somebody in your household. This technology means that you're free from the need to go to a particular place to work and, for some roles, that you can also be free from the need to do your work between set hours.

Now find your own way – get flexible!

FREAKS – CONTROL AND OTHER

The word 'freak' was originally – in the sixteenth century – about capriciousness or a sudden, causeless, change of mind. But by the nineteenth and twentieth centuries a different meaning had emerged. The word began to be used to describe a monstrosity or an abnormally developed individual. Change has continued and we now have 'phone phreaks', who use electronic devices to get free telephone calls and people who 'freak out', casting off what they think are old-fashioned ways of thinking, dressing and behaving.

But none of these describe the sort of freaks that we get in our organizations. These are difficult to spot because they don't dress differently (*see* **Dressing Up and Dressing Down**), they behave in ways that appear to be 'normal' and they blend into the corporate 'wallpaper'. But you'll detect them by their obsessions. These are magnificent. They cause these freaks repeatedly to perform acts that appear – to you – to be meaningless; they are the result of hidden, often dark compulsions. Getting on the wrong side of these freaks can drop your survival rating. So here are some notes to help you to identify the freaks of your organization:

The control freak

The commonest form of organizational freak, this is often, but not always, found in large organizations. Control freaks are obsessed by their need to control you and what you do. People with the more extreme form of this obsession are said to have a desire to control *everything*. In attempting to do this they will create things like questionnaires, audits, reviews, procedures and checklists. The aim of these is to generate the information that they think they need in order to control you. They often have job titles (*see* **Job Titles**) that include words like co-ordinator, controller or auditor. Once they have you in their sights, control freaks are difficult, if not impossible, to shake off. The most effective tactics seem to be either to cut your losses and fill in the questionnaire or to suggest that it's time for them or their department to be audited.

The power freak

The power freak is a relatively rare form of organizational freak. It has been suggested that the reason for this is their high mortality rate – a result of the enemies they make as they climb over all and sundry on their way to more and more organizational power. However, recent studies appear to indicate that it may be the obsession – for power – rather than the person, that's short-lived (*see* **Thirty-Five Plus**). Avoiding the power freak is almost impossible – all you can do is hope that the damage they create as they climb up and over you is limited.

The money freak

An overwhelming obsession with money is what marks the money freak out from the rest of us. Created in early childhood by a confusion between money and love or affection this obsession causes the money freak to develop tunnel vision about money. When you say 'That's a great idea', in response to something new, the money freak asks 'But how much will it cost?' But money freaks don't just exist in Accountancy departments. They can appear all over the organization and are often described as having 'a keen eye for the bottom line issues' (*see* **Buzzwords**) – none of which makes any sense except, of course, to a money freak. The trick with money freaks is to use them to your advantage rather than try and defeat them. After all, somebody has to count the beans!

The techno freak

The techno freaks of our organizations are obsessed with technology. If it's not computers that they home in on, then it'll be conference calling, WAP portal phones, satellite data linkages or web sites. While technology undoubtedly has its uses, what you have to decide is whether it's useful to you and useful *now*. The techno freak lacks the ability to make that decision. To him or her it's technology, new-glossy-exciting-go-faster technology and that, to the techno freak, means that it's *good*. But techno freaks do have their uses. These days, most of you have more technology then you can cope with. This means that the techno freaks are definitely 'in'. So use them to help you find your way through all this technology – but don't expect to understand what they say.

The word 'friend' gets used – and misused – a lot. Some of these uses are unique and special, as in the House of Commons of the British Parliament where members address each other as 'my right honourable friend' or in the English law courts where lawyers will address each other as 'my learned friend'. But when you use this word in your ordinary, everyday speech, its use can be inconsistent and contradictory. For example, you'll use 'friend' to describe someone that you know well or work closely with. You'll also use it when you speak to someone who's a casual acquaintance or even a stranger, usually to signal goodwill or kindly intention on your part. Friend is also, from time to time, used to mean a lover, someone who wishes you well, a sympathizer, favourer, helper, patron, or supporter and, of course, as the opposite of enemy. Most, if not all, of these meanings are used in organizations on a day-by-day basis.

Sadly, most of you don't have or get the sort of friends that you really deserve. You have to make do with the sort of conditional 'half friendships' that arise in the enforced intimacy of a workplace in which you didn't choose the people that you work with. For some of you this is a source of disappointment, even resentment. For others, the realization that friends aren't really friends (and might even be enemies) is a challenge and an obstacle to be overcome (*see* **Betrayal**). But among the rest of you are those for whom a friendship – whatever its nature or origins – is an opportunity. It's one that might just lead to mutual trust and caring (*see* **Trust**; **Caring**). If it does – if you become *real* friends – then you've both got something that's incredibly important in your struggle to survive in your organization. A friend like this is, as Dr Johnson told us, someone to whom you are joined 'in mutual benevolence and intimacy'. This sort of friend is, like a good boss, a rare occurrence (*see* **Bosses – Good**). When they do enter your life they should be nurtured. For they will help and support you through all the ups and downs of your organizational life. They'll listen to you, challenge you, tell you jokes, share their secrets with you, and laugh at and with you. In short, they'll be your friend.

The games we played as children were for fun or the joy of learning and exercising a particular skill or talent. The games that are played in our organizations are very different. These are serious, heavy duty affairs with only one aim – that of winning. Most of these organizational games are about dominance or territory – and occasionally both (*see* **Dominance**). Dominance involves who's where in the pecking order – it's about things like position at the feeding trough or influence (*see* **Pecking Order**). But territory isn't about land or the physical assets of an organization. Most of the time it's about control of information or decisions. The rules of these organizational games range from the simple and nominal – such as 'Don't trust anybody' – to the complexity of time-worn rituals acted out between old opponents – 'We never agree with Marketing!'

> *'Game, noun: an unserious occupation designed for the relaxation of busy people and the distraction of idle ones; it's used to take people to whom we have nothing to say off our hands, and sometimes even ourselves.'*
>
> Etienne Bonnot

But if you step back from the detail of these games you'll see that three basic and common factors begin to emerge. These are that the games of your organization, are: (a) repetitive in nature; (b) about winning or losing; and (c) very similar to the 'games' played out in collectives of animals such as baboons, wolves and lions. The challenge of changing this situation is not a new one. These repetitive dominance-driven games have been around for a long time. But they are now of growing importance. The organizations that survive the firestorms of change of the twenty-first century will be those who find effective alternatives to the win–lose games of hormonally-driven alpha males and females. Talk to your co-workers about this and, with them, try to create some new games that are about learning, enjoyable, unique, about win–win outcomes, and, above all about working together. You've nothing to lose but a bit of dignity and you might find that you gain the real buzz of working in an effective and well integrated team (*see* **Teams**).

GLASS CEILINGS

The phrase 'glass ceiling' was first used in March 1986 in the *Wall Street Journal*. It described the invisible barrier that blocks the upward progress of women in organizations. Now, decades later, it still has the same meaning. But it's also been joined by other demonstrations of this inequality. For now there are:

■ 'glass walls' – the horizontal barriers in organisations that prevent employees from moving between functional areas or from service divisions into line management, and

■ 'sticky floors' – meaning no career movement beyond the initial entry job.

All of these are examples of the inequality of access and opportunity suffered by women and minorities. They are the artificial barriers that deny, on the grounds of gender or race, talented, well qualified, people the opportunity to advance their careers (*see* **Racism**).

There has been little real change in the decades that have passed since these barriers were first identified. The prejudices and attitudes of senior managers continue to limit women's opportunities, particularly for those women with children or caring responsibilities. Survey after survey tells of intelligent, experienced and capable women whose careers come to a halt because they get married or have children.

All of this comes about because of attitudes and prejudices that are deeply embedded in the culture of many of our organizations (*see* **Archaeology – Corporate**). These are the organizations with paternalistic white male managers and 'jobs-for-the-boys' attitudes to recruitment and promotion. They haven't adjusted to the new environment of 'managing your own career' and merit-based promotion. As a result, women make up less than 10 per cent of executive directors in the UK and less than 5 per cent of senior managers in US Fortune 1000 and 500 companies. Only 15 per cent of women employed by the top 75 organizations of the Australian finance sector are managers and administrators.

But there is some hope. More and more women can be found in junior and middle management, more companies are introducing formal measures to ensure equality for all staff irrespective of age (*see* **Ageism**), gender or race (*see* **Racism**), and more and more governments are introducing laws that make discrimination on these grounds illegal.

In the meantime, for those of you who find yourselves disadvantaged because you are a woman or come from a minority group, here are some guidelines:

■ Check out the way others around you behave; think about the rules and regulations of your workplace. Have the courage (*see* **Courage**) to speak out if you think these are racist or discriminatory.

■ Keep a record of incidents involving racism or discrimination – log what was said or done, dates, times, details and witnesses.

■ Confront direct discrimination or racism. Tell the person involved quietly, politely but assertively (*see* **Assertion**) that you take issue with their behaviour and that should it happen again you'll make a formal complaint.

■ If you can't manage doing that on your own, check (quietly and discreetly) with other people in your workplace. You may find that you've more support than you thought you had. You may even find that others are suffering too. If that's so, then take action as a group.

■ If your confrontation hasn't worked then take the evidence that you've gathered to an independent third party. Make sure that it's someone with power and make sure that the information that you give them is objective, factual and untainted by any suggestion of ambition or malice on your part.

■ Remember, *nobody* has the right to discriminate against you because of your race or gender.

'I thought you said we had an equal opportunity policy.'

GO – NO-GO

It's been quite a while since pioneer American astronaut John Glenn told Mission Control 'I am go; all systems are go'. But that choice – Go or No-Go – is one that's still with us. You may not realize it but you face the same choice every day – you're either Go or you're No-Go. There are no perhaps's or maybes – it's a clear-cut, black or white choice.

Go is about:

- taking the risk;
- riding the waves of change;
- embracing uncertainty;
- reaching out into the unknown;
- looking for opportunity;
- living for growth;
- growing to live;
- defining your own goals – ones that stretch you;
- developing and honing your skills;
- sometimes making mistakes – but always learning.

While No-Go is locked into:

- seeing change as a threat;
- hanging on to certainty in an uncertain world;
- keeping to the known and secure;
- living for safety;
- limiting your risk – and your goals;
- being an expert – who never, ever gets it wrong.

The choice is yours – which are you going to choose?

GOOD – AND BAD – HAIR DAYS

When the phrase 'I'm having a bad hair day' first came into common usage it was mainly used by women and was, literally, about the state of their hair. Now, things are different. The use of this phrase has not only spread into the male side of our organizations, it's also changed its meaning. It's now a comment on or an explanation of how you feel. You use it to tell your co-workers that you're feeling low, ill-at-ease with yourself, less confident or not as sociable as you usually are. As such it's become an expression that reflects the state of your self-esteem. When this is low you're having a bad hair day, and when it's high you're having a good hair day. The more you think about this, the easier it is to understand. For your hair is an important aspect of the way you look – and the better you look, the better you feel. So it's really not at all surprising to find that a comment you make about a key part of your appearance is really an expression of your state of mind.

So what can you do if you're having a bad hair day or – to put it another way, your self-esteem is low? If this is an infrequent and occasional event then you shouldn't worry about it too much. All of us have down days and it may just be your turn. But if your bad hair days get to be frequent and persistent events then you need to start looking at what's happening around you and how you feel about that. Check out whether you're being subjected to low-level but persistent harassment or bullying (*see* **Bullying**; **Harassment**) and run the rule over your stress levels to see if they've been creeping up (*see* **Winding Up and Winding Down**). If you get a 'yes' on either of these then don't delay – act

> 'The good life is a process, not a state of being. It is a direction, not a destination.'
>
> Carl Rogers

now, do something about it before having a bad hair day gets to be a habit. If doing something on your own is difficult then get some help. In the long run, it's better if you get help that's both skilled, professionally trained and not connected to your workplace. The skilled professional independent counsellor will work with you to help you identify and resolve the issues that are giving you your 'bad hair days'.

GOSSIP

Organizations are people and, wherever you find people, you'll find gossip. Gossip is like a drop of oil on a puddle or pond – it spreads easily and quickly. Gossip can be malicious, critical, vindictive, affectionate, humorous or caring. Few of you will be able to say that you don't gossip. Surprisingly, the dictionary underrates gossip, describing it as 'idle talk; trifling or groundless rumour; tittle-tattle'. But gossip is more than that. For gossip is the way that you guess about and try to make sense of what you see going on around you. You'll gossip about many things: the ways in which you see others doing – or not doing – their jobs, the rumoured reorganization, the hinted-at promotions or demotions, the clothes that someone is wearing or why Fred never brings his wife to company social events.

Whatever its content, your gossip is your attempt to assess the ways in which you see others behaving. When you are uneasy, even fearful of their actions, your gossip is critical. You gossip when you think others are behaving in ways that are different or 'not normal'.

> *'Gossip is the mechanism we use in response to the inevitable separateness of our individual lives.'*
> Susie Orbach

You'll wonder at the reasons for this – and pass judgement. You'll gossip when someone behaves in ways that you admire or wish to imitate. This gossip isn't just about trying to understand those actions, it's also about exploring your fascination for or admiration of what they have done. You also try to gauge whether you should or could emulate them. But gossip, whatever its focus or direction, is also about probing, testing and assessing the reactions of the people with whom you gossip. For when you gossip, you not only test how you feel about the subject in hand, you also explore how others feel about it. This sort of gossip plays an important role in the way that the unwritten 'rules' of organizations evolve (*see* **Unwritten Rules**), and can enforce those 'rules' by applying social pressure. Whatever you do will be gossiped about. Try to learn to live with it and use it to your advantage.

The word 'grapevine' first came into common use during the American civil war. As a shortened version of the phrase 'a despatch by grape-vine telegraph' it was used to describe a rumour. Nowadays, it's also used to tell you about the quality of information – as in 'I heard on the grapevine that . . .'. Grapevines are important. They are informal – but often very extensive – word-of-mouth message networks that transmit information very quickly. They also provide connections that would be very difficult, or even impossible, to achieve through more formal channels.

All of this tells you that the grapevine is a very powerful way of communicating. It will tell you about the about-to-happen sacking, the pay rise and the takeover – and often at what seems to be the speed of light. But the grapevine's message can change. Bits are added on to it or taken off it; they might even have changed completely. This is the 'Chinese whispers' or 'Telephone tag' phenomenon where the longer the message chain, the more distorted the message will become. If you want to prove this there's a children's party game that involves getting six or more children to whisper a single sentence message to each other down a line and then laugh at how different it's become by the end. In your organization the messages or rumours that get sent on the grapevine are often much more complex than those of this game and – not surprisingly – they get distorted. But despite this you can use the grapevine in your attempts to find out about and influence your new boss (*see* **Bosses – New**), or to support your actions as an 'agent for change' (*see* **Bosses – Not So Good**) or just to find out what's happening (*see* **Gossip**). So, if you're going to use the grapevine – and there's no reason why you shouldn't – here are some tips:

- ■ Don't put anything that you value on the grapevine.
- ■ Make sure that your message is straightforward and short.
- ■ Try to launch the message onto the grapevine as close to your 'target' as you can.
- ■ Package your message so that it's interesting and worth passing on.
- ■ Be prepared to have the message changed, distorted or even lost in transit.

Towards the end of the twentieth century *The Economist* magazine asked a number of people to do some crystal ball gazing. They were asked to predict what would happen to a number of economic variables over the following decade. The variables were:

■ £ versus US$ value;

■ the price of oil;

■ the rate of inflation;

■ Singapore's gross domestic output.

The people asked included multinational senior executives, Oxford University students, government finance ministers and refuse collectors. Most of us would have expected the best predictions to be made by the multinational executives or the finance ministers. But, a decade later, it was the lowly refuse collectors who'd produced the best predictions for most of these key economic factors!

This ability to see further than we can is just one of the qualities that we expect from our management gurus. We also expect them to tell us what is 'right' or 'wrong' – in terms of what it takes to ensure success – and what we must do in order to gain that success. Their influence can be extraordinary. Organization after organization grasps and swallows piecemeal the words of these often charismatic individuals as if they had been brought down from Mount Olympus. These organizations then restructure, re-engineer, refocus or repackage themselves, often at the cost of people's jobs (*see* **Downsizing**). So, given that recent history tells us that all of this can affect our chances of surviving in our organization, let's take a look at what these gurus do and why it is that what they give us is so attractive.

To be a successful management guru you seem to need the following:

■ a *big* idea – preferably original but, if not, then repackaged so it looks and sounds different;

■ the ability to put this idea in a contemporary context and make it seem relevant;

■ the ability to bring order out of chaos, or at least appear to;

- the ability to illuminate the darker, less predictable and less frequently visited corners of our organizations;
- the ability to do all of this at the same time as standing up in front of a large audience; and
- a publishing contract.

Doing all of this – doing it well – seems to bring structure and meaning into the day-to-day lives of those who control our organizations. Such knowledge is reassuring – it adds certainty and reduces risk. But be warned! For the success of the ten-year predictions of *The Economist*'s refuse collectors tells us of the dangers that lurk in unconditional acceptance of a guru's declarations.

But have gurus always been like this? When you probe further into history you'll find there is a much older and world-wide tradition of spiritual gurus or teachers. This has much to give us. This tradition has been around for several thousand years, rather than the half century of our western management gurus. They also have an approach which is radically different from that of our management gurus. For these gurus, in order to be effective in their teaching, used (and still do use) methods and means that were quite unconventional. These were often so different that they would be seen as outrageous by the standards of conventional religion. These 'holy fools' and 'crazy adepts' instructed others in ways that were designed to shock and challenge the conventional, and inevitably static, ways of seeing the world. In so doing they enabled their followers to gain new insights and so gain access to different ways of seeing the world around them. Applying this approach to the organizations of the twenty-first century means abandoning the safe and conventional ways of managing. It means experimenting with newer, less conventional ways which challenge the people of our organizations to use their skills and creativity rather than 'do it by the book'. Be warned, though, for if you abandon the ways of the conventional management gurus not only will you challenge the people with whom you work, you'll also challenge your own view of what you do and don't do in your organization.

Why not start tomorrow – by getting your work group to tell you what they'd like to achieve before they go home. Be prepared for some surprises!

Being harassed is a very common experience – both in and out of organizations. It happens when managers lack the basic skills to manage you (*see* **Bosses – Not So Good**), when supervisors decide to take a short-cut route to your compliance or when other people decide that they know better than you. Harassment is a close cousin of bullying (*see* **Bullying**) but one that's subtler, less 'in-your-face' than that form of domination (*see* **Dominance**). For while bullying draws heavily on the act of physical domination, harassment acts through your emotions. It's an act that's aimed at influencing the way that you feel. When you're harassed you're harried, vexed or troubled by repeated small and covert attacks. The harasser aims to wear you down or out, to tire or exhaust you. You're worried, mentally and repeatedly, by your harasser, just as a dog will worry at a toy or a cat will play with a mouse. Because of this, harassment is often more difficult to pin down. For example, a harasser will say, in defence of his or her actions: 'No, of course I didn't intend to worry you when I suggested that you consider early retirement' or 'I was trying to be considerate when I suggested we discuss your mistakes' – all of which seem perfectly reasonable – on the surface.

So how do you cope with harassment? The first thing you can do is to make sure that it doesn't get you down while the second thing is to turn to face it – or rather, the harasser – rather than fleeing from her or him. Here are some other ideas for you to try, ideas that have stood the test of time and the harassing workplace:

- Use humour – turn what the harasser says into a joke. When they don't think it's funny just tell them that you were only teasing.
- Ignore it.
- Develop an automatic response that turns the harassment aside – a *Mona Lisa* smile with a built-in grunt might work.
- Share what you feel is happening with your co-workers and try to arrange things so that they witness what's happening.
- Find out if it's happening to anybody else. If it is, then let the harasser know – assertively (*see* **Assertion**) – that you're on to him or her and that if it doesn't stop you'll be making a joint formal complaint.

- Try to cut down on the amount of harassment by not being alone with the harasser.
- Look after yourself – being harassed is stressful.
- Find out if your employer has a policy on harassment or guidelines on what sort of behaviour is – and isn't – acceptable in the workplace.
- If none of the above works, gather evidence about the sort of things that are being said – witnesses are very useful – and then take it to an independent third party such as an official of your labour union or an equal opportunities manager. You might even need to draw upon the support of your pastor or priest. Whoever you use, *do* make sure that the formal complaint that you make to them is objective, factual and untainted by any suggestion of ambition or malice on your part.
- Remember, you *do not* have to put up with being harassed.

HOW NOT TO No. 5: MORE PEOPLE CARE

Jane's mother had died at the end of a long and, for Jane, stressful three years of decline; years during which her mother had drifted further and further out of touch with reality and become less and less able to communicate. Jane took the five days of 'compassionate leave' the rule book allowed her and came back to work shortly after the funeral. In her office she found flowers and cards – from Ruth, the manager she shared an office with, the team leaders, even from the secretarial staff. As she sat at her desk looking at them she realized that there wasn't anything from Rachel, the senior manager. 'She must be busy', Jane thought, remembering Rachel had been the first to be told – Jane had had a meeting scheduled with her for the day after her mother had died. Jane tidied the cards away, started work on the pile of paperwork that was waiting.

When the phone rang, it was Rachel. Her voice sounded cool, distant, as she asked Jane to come down to her office – now. 'Now you're back at work, there's something I want to say to you.' Rachel's eyes matched her voice – grey, distant and impersonal. 'We think that you ought to consider early retirement, the terms can be very good you know.'

'Hope is a waking dream.'

Aristotle

'Hope is the risk that must be run.'

Georges Bernanos

'If it were not for hope, the heart would break.'

Thomas Fuller

'We should not let our fears hold us back from pursuing our hopes.'

John F. Kennedy

'Hope has as many lives as a cat or a king.'

Longfellow

'Hope deferred makes the heart sick.'

Proverbs 13:12

'Hope for the best.'

Proverb

'Hope springs eternal in the human breast.'

Alexander Pope

'Hope is good breakfast but a bad supper.'

W. Rawley

'Hope is essential to both the business of living and the life of business'

Anon

'. . . you discover more about a person when you learn about his hopes than when you count his achievements, for the best of what we are lies in what we hope to be.'

A.C. Grayling

'Hopefulness is crucial when anyone undertakes a tough task; positive expectations may be especially beneficial in the toughest jobs, where high optimism may be a pragmatic job strategy.'

Daniel Goleman

INCREDIBLE SHRINKING CHIPS

It wasn't that long ago that computers were slow and limited in capacity. They were housed in special rooms with air conditioning and usually surrounded by a priesthood of IT specialists who knew the special languages or codes needed for access. Computers were inaccessible, difficult to use and not remotely personal. The incredible shrinking chip has blown this all away and you now have computers that are accessible and are easy to use.

These computers are beginning to be personal – rather than corporate. You can decide the 'how' and 'for what' of their use and their software reflects your needs rather than those of your organization. If you are a technophile then none of this will be news to you. But if you're not remotely interested in the RAMs, ROMs, CPUs and GUIs (*see* **Acronyms**) of the computer world – but just want better tools with which to do your job – what then can the computer do for you and your survival rating? Here are some answers:

- Never forget that, contrary to appearances, even the latest and glitziest computer is really just an expensive, fast, stupid adding machine.
- Only use a computer if it gives you benefits.
- Always, always back up your work – *especially* if it's really important!
- Remember that your new computer *will* be obsolete within six months.
- Obsolete doesn't equal useless – it's what your computer does for *you* that counts.

If you let it, your computer will help you to do more – quickly and productively. But none of that is guaranteed, unless you contribute your own skills, abilities and creativity to balance the equation.

INFLUENCE – OR POWER?

For some of you, influence and power are the buzz that you get from your organization. They're what you joined up for; they're what you strive and lust after. But this isn't true for everybody. After all, influence and power have to be used on somebody and we can't all be in charge. But what's the difference between them and how, if at all, can you use them to raise your survival rating?

It is easy to get confused between influence and power. They're both commonly used – often interchangeably – when you talk about and describe the sorts of things that go on in your organizations. You describe people as being powerful and you say that somebody else appears to exert influence over events or people. But when you look them up in the dictionary you'll find that differences begin to emerge. The *Oxford English Dictionary* tells you, for example, that power is 'the ability to do or effect something or anything, or to act upon a person or thing'. It also tells you that influence is about 'the exercise of personal power by human beings'. Another way to look at this is to say that power is the stuff that enables you to influence someone. That is it enables you to change either what they do or think.

But what is this stuff called power and where does it come from? You'll have power for a number of reasons. You can be powerful because of the role or job that you have – position power; the resources that you control – resource power; the information that you have access to – information power; the expertise that you possess – expert power; or because of your charisma or personality – personal power. Almost everyone has some sort of power. What's different is:

■ the sort of power that you have,

■ how much of it you've got, and

■ how you use it.

See if you can work out what sort of power your boss and co-workers have got and how they use it. Of course, having that power is only half the story. What's also important is the way that you use – or abuse – it and the ends or outcomes that you use it towards. For example, while being a supervisor or group leader gives you role power, this is often extended by the expert power that your experience gives you and the information power that authorized access to the systems of the organization and your connections with other supervisors and managers give you. You can either use all this power to dominate and coerce your work group – and hence appear to protect your position in the organization – or you can use it to manage the group using participation and consensus (*see* **Consensus**) – and hence develop the people in it. Having power and using it well is obviously useful in an organization. It enables you to influence people and that influence – if you get it right – will enable you to do more and better things.

When you look at the sorts of words that are used to describe the ways that you and your co-workers influence each other you'll find there's quite a variety. For example, you can – and regularly do – educate, persuade, seduce, manipulate, propagandize, subvert or coerce each other. But when you look more closely at these words you begin to see something else. For they range from those that are done *with* you – as in education or training – to those that are done *to* you – as in coercion. In your workplace, for example, bullying and harassment are forms of coercion that are done *to* people, while training can only produce results when it is done *with* those people (*see* **Bullying**; **Harassment**; **Training**).

But all of these ways of exerting influence have something in common. For they all act on your freedom to control your life, your individual autonomy. They all strive to adjust, modify and convert that autonomy. When you train or educate others, for example, you offer them the opportunity to acquire knowledge. Once acquired, that knowledge can be used in ways that are autonomous – that is as they choose to use it. At the other end of this spectrum when you force or coerce others to do what you want, you say 'Do this – or else!' – and leave them little or no opportunity to exercise their autonomy, to do what they think is right. All of the other influence processes – seduction, manipulation, propaganda and subversion – have, as your experience will tell you, their own distinctive ways and means of influencing your autonomy.

Recognizing and nurturing your own source of power and learning to use it in ways that are positive are both very important to your survival in your organization. Get them wrong and you'll lose both of them, get them right and you'll gain even more!

INSTITUTIONALIZATION

Many organizations can be described as institutions. As such they are a long-lasting feature of the political, social or economic life of the community. These organizations are all set up or created with a particular objective in mind. That objective can be about almost anything. It can be commercial, religious or charitable in nature, concerned with education or particular political views or focused on the provision of a public or general utility (*see* **Organizations**). Many of you spend your working lives in these institutions. You do this because working there gives you a sense of security, a sort of social life and provides an answer to the pressing need to earn a living. But what can – and does – happen when you do this is that you become institutionalized.

Institutionalization is a state of mind. It's one that comes about when you are persistently exposed to a certain sort of social environment. It's the sort of environment in which:

- you are treated as if you are incapable of taking an active or responsible role, and
- in which your social interactions are controlled and limited by the needs and rules of the institution or organization – rather than your own needs.

Extreme institutionalization is very common among long-stay prisoners and children who have been raised in inadequately staffed care homes. It causes erosion or loss of personal identity – that this-is-who-I-am feeling – and leads to a feeling that your life isn't under your control anymore.

But these aren't the only places where institutionalization occurs. For we are all subject to the pressure to conform. This pressure to act in ways that are controlled and for the good of the institution, is present whatever the nature or purpose of your organization. It can be overt and in-your-face – as in formal written rules and procedures – or covert and insidious – as in unwritten rules or corporate cultures (*see* **Unwritten Rules; Dressing Up and Dressing Down**). It can be enforced by punishment and penalties or by social pressure (*see* **You're In – or You're Out**). When these begin to erode your freedom of individual choice they become the leading edge of *your* institutionalization. If you're not sure as to whether institutionalization is present in your organization then take a look around you. See if you can see any of these symptoms in your co-workers or bosses: lack of social know-how, difficulty with peer group relationships, attention-seeking behaviour, aggression (*see* **Aggression**), temper tantrums, lack of eye or touch contact. If you do spot some of these symptoms in your organization, remember that institutionalization isn't infectious, nor is it inevitable. Here are some of the things that you can do to keep institutionalization at bay:

◼ learn to say 'no' – but with grace and style;
◼ keep your personal options open;
◼ wear a red shirt or blouse on dressing-down days;
◼ ask for vegan food to be served in the canteen;
◼ sing a song – occasionally;
◼ say 'why?' as often as you dare.

'Of course . . . we encourage individuality.'

The phrase 'jack of all trades' is one that's often used to describe somebody with a wide range of competencies. The words 'competence' and 'competency' are turning up quite a lot these days. A competence is a behaviour that's needed in order to achieve the objectives of the organization – rather than your individual objectives. Your job is often described in terms of its *key* competencies – those that you *must* have if you're to do that job well. These are often obvious and generalized: communication, leadership, judgement, initiative, motivation, analytic skills, planning, innovation, interpersonal skills and numeracy are all examples. These and other competencies are usually clumped together under the equally generalized headings of:

- individual competencies – such as flexibility, tenacity or risk-taking;
- interpersonal competencies – like persuasiveness and communication;
- analytical competencies – such as problem solving and numeracy;
- managerial competencies – such as leadership, control and planning;
- motivational competencies – such as resilience, stamina and drive.

But when you really look at these lists – rather than just accept them – you'll soon find yourself asking some questions. Where, for example, are the competencies that make your working days enjoyable?; Where are those key behaviours that help you to really understand each other or move you to offer help or support to a co-worker? Where are those basic human qualities like compassion, caring or conviction? The answer comes when you remind yourself that a competency is a behaviour that is necessary to achieve the objectives of the organization. Bear that in mind when you're writing your next job advert or when you're interviewing your next job applicant. It won't do any harm if, when you're doing that, you ask yourself questions like 'Is this the sort of person who's likely to burst into song when he or she's happy?' or 'Would he visit a co-worker who's house-bound by illness or accident?', or 'Would she stay back to help a co-worker who's overloaded?'.

These are the competencies that make us human beings, these are our *real* competencies.

If you look up the word 'jargon' in the dictionary you'll find that it has a number of meanings. But the one that's most relevant to your survival rating is the one that tells you that jargon is: 'any mode of speech abounding in unfamiliar terms, or peculiar to a particular set of persons'. This sort of jargon gets used in the workplace for a number of reasons. It can, for example, be a specialist 'shorthand' that gets used by a limited and specialist group. Here's an example:

'The solubility of tin in the alpha solid solution rises to 13.5% at 798°C. At this temperature a peritectic reaction occurs resulting in the formation of a beta intermediate solid solution.'

For this to make any sense you need to have specialized knowledge of metallurgy and be familiar with the specialist words (or jargon) involved. This sort of jargon can be very effective but *only* if the people who are listening to it or reading it have that specialized knowledge.

But most of the time you don't meet that sort of jargon. What you do meet is the sort of jargon that people use when they want you to think that they know more than you do. Here's an example: 'Taking a helicopter view of the situation, I think we're looking at some pretty wild and blue-sky stuff here.' This sort of jargon doesn't rate very high on the communication stakes. Its meaning – that what's being discussed is high risk and speculative – is inaccessible, almost lost. For the uninitiated it's annoying and confusing and when you use it you run the risk that people will think that you're a pretentious show-off – rather than an up-to-date 'whizz-kid.'

But jargon can and does have an 'up-side'. Using it with people who also understand and use it can emphasize your membership of a group. It can give you that warm feeling that comes from being an 'insider'. But be warned, for when you use this sort of jargon you're excluding others (*see* **You're In – or You're Out**).

Titles, particularly job titles, are important. They're about rank, status and position and they're often seen by others as a guide to where you stand on the power ladder of your organization (*see* **Pecking Order**). As soon as you hear what somebody's job title is you slot them into a pigeon-hole. They say 'I'm a secretary' or 'I'm a director' and when you hear that you attach a label to them – a label drawn from a rich library of social stereotypes. With this label comes a whole package of preconceived and oversimplified ideas about how they might or might not behave and what they do and don't do.

But, like the rest of the work-a-day world, job titles are changing. A road cleaner is now a sanitation technician, a salesperson has become a face-to-face representative, a secretary has changed into an information co-ordinator, and the office 'gofer' – who does the photocopying and changes the toner cartridge – is transformed into a reprographics operator. Some of these changes come about because of the tides of supply and demand in the job market. They make the job sound more attractive and, hence, more fillable. But that's not the only reason why job titles are changing. The workplace has changed; what a secretary or director did twenty years ago is very different from what she – or he – does now. Some newer organizations seem able to cope with this. In the Ben & Jerry's ice-cream company you'll find titles like 'serving supremo' or 'flavourmeister'. Some organizations go as far as allowing their staff to choose their own job titles. Try it out – see if you can come up with four or five words that *really* identify what you do best; what the unique spark is that *you* bring to your workplace. Write it down in the box below. Revisit it every week to make sure that it still fits. After all, you're going to change, expand and develop and if the job box you're in is flexible enough to go with you, then you'll need to change your job title. But if that doesn't happen and you find yourself banging up against the walls of the prison that your job has become, then it's time to think about moving on (*see* **To Boldly Go**; **Your Future**; **Résumés and Other Stories**).

My real job title is:

KNOWLEDGE WORKER

'It's not what you know – it's what you do with it that matters' is one of those sayings that have been around for a long time. But in the twenty-first century knowledge *is* power and becoming a knowledge worker is a key step in your plan for survival. But what is a knowledge worker and how is she or he different from the rest of the people in your organization?

At its core, knowledge management isn't just about amassing huge quantities of data, it's about knowing what to do with that data, knowing how to convert it into information and, most importantly, knowing how to use that information. These days, most data is IT based. This gives you the first part of the answer to the above question. For IT literacy is a must for you to be an effective knowledge worker. But that literacy must have a focus – it's not enough for you to be a purely passive information conduit. You'll start to get a clue as to what that focus must be when you look at the way that information technology has lead to increasing numbers of the people-tasks – tasks routinely or traditionally done by people – are becoming 'programmable' and hence 'do-able' by IT systems. This opens a door for you, through which you can see the opportunity for synergy between your ability to create and innovate and the information processing abilities of IT systems. But only a few will pass through that door. Those who do – the knowledge workers of the twenty-first century – will have jobs that are about making sure that their organizations are 'doing the right thing', rather than being locked into 'doing things right'. To achieve that you've got to find, or create, an organization in which sharing knowledge is an integral part of everybody's job, one in which performance *and* learning are rewarded. On the way to finding or founding that organization you've got to:

- make sure that you keep abreast with advances in new technology;
- learn to see your organization 'in the round';
- develop learning and decision-taking skills;
- network, network and network;
- learn to manage your own workload;
- sharpen up your team-working skills;
- become a risk taker.

Most of you, if asked, would say that you are logical. You work out things from what you observe and you do so in a way that is 'straight-line' and reasonable. When you do that, your attention moves smoothly from one thought to another, each of these being in a chain with preceding and following partners. An example of this is: 'All whales are mammals and all mammals are warm-blooded, so all whales are warm-blooded.' When you think in this sort of way, which is often called 'vertical' thinking, you are being selective. You make judgements about what you do – and don't – include in your thinking, judgements based on proof and some sense of what is 'right' and 'wrong'. This vertical thinking looks for answers that are unique and 'right' and uses information only for its value or its meaning in the process of looking for that answer.

Lateral thinking is different. It looks for what is different, rather than what is right or wrong, and uses information to trigger new ideas. Chance intrusions are welcome in lateral thinking; it's a process that's about discovering new ways of looking at things. Here's an example:

Question: How do you reduce supermarket theft?

Answer 1:   Weigh customers when they enter and when they leave and charge on basis of the difference in weights.

Answer 2:   Vary price discounts on weekly basis to reflect theft rate – more theft, less discount and less theft, more discount.

Answer 3:   Make all food free but charge for entry.

Lateral thinking has two basic processes. First, it asks you to escape from ideas and concepts that dominate or polarize your thinking. It demands that you free yourself from the prison of the 'right' answer; it asks you to undo the strait-jacket of conventional thinking. Second, it asks you to provoke your thinking by allowing yourself to be 'wrong', by making unjustified leaps, by using an idea as catalyst rather than an answer and by keeping idea generation separate from idea evaluation. Lateral thinking is about unlocking your creativity. As such it is usually used with, rather than as a substitute for, vertical thinking, with ideas being generated by lateral thinking and then evaluated by vertical thinking.

Try it out for yourself!

LAUGHTER

Laughter first entered your life when you were about one month old. By the time you were three months of age it had taken up permanent residence. Laughter is universal and powerful. Everybody laughs. It comes in response to both the familiar and the unfamiliar, is used to attract attention, to express relief and to announce uncertainty. But, most of all, you laugh when you find something funny. Each of you laughs in a unique way; you each have a very individual combination of facial expression, physical movement and noise that go to make up *your* laugh. Genuine humorous laughter is good for you. Not only does it make you feel better, more alive, but it also boosts your immune system and triggers off biochemical changes in your body that are the reverse of those that happen when you become too stressed (*see* **Winding Up and Winding Down**). So why is it then that you don't see – or rather hear – more of it in your organization?

Part of the answer to this lies in the fact that laughter isn't always socially acceptable. Audible laughter has, from time to time, been described as being 'ill-bred', 'the mind sneezing', 'the hiccup of a fool' and its presence has been said to speak of 'a vacant mind'. The way that laughter is described goes on to give you more clues about what's going on here. You say that you 'cracked up', 'split your sides', 'convulsed yourself', even 'wet yourself' or 'died' laughing. All of these are descriptions of being out of control. This is confirmed when you watch someone *really* laughing. You see bulging eyes, body movements that involve shaking and spasming, unusual facial expressions that expose teeth and tongue, hyperventilation, weeping, exaggerated head and shoulder movements and strange, loud, spasmodic, trumpeting sounds. This tells you that you're looking at a human being who is, albeit momentarily, out of control. This is why you don't hear laughter in your organization. For when you laugh like that – a real laugh rather than a polite social titter – you expose yourself and by doing that you put yourself at risk.

But, despite all this, and despite its absence from your organization, humorous laughter is definitely here to stay. For humour brings you and your co-workers closer together, it confirms and strengthens your relationships, it shows you what you share – rather than what divides you – and, above all, it's universal. All of these are things that will increase your survival rating and help you to survive your organization.

Once upon a time, not so very long ago, people thought that the world was divided into two groups of people: those who led and those who followed. The first of these, the 'leader' group, was almost exclusively male and made up of people who were born into the job. These leaders were seen to have certain special character 'traits' or ways of behaving. This view – that leaders are born and not made – persisted for a long time. Much research was aimed at finding out exactly what was the magic 'formula' that turned a person into a leader. But all of this failed. There was no magic 'formula'. In the meantime the world had changed. People – men *and* women – were finding leadership thrust upon them in an astonishingly wide variety of situations – and they were managing to lead successfully without the benefit of birthright.

Nowadays, most people are more open about this business of leadership. As a consequence there are many views about how leading ought to be carried out. While the good thing about this is that it gets you away from the 'leaders are born' school of thought, the bad thing is that it can be confusing. However, there is a sort of consensus. This tells us that what is appropriate – in leadership terms – depends upon a number of things. Amongst the more significant of these you'll find such things as:

- where the leading is being done – a battlefield, or office, workshop, boardroom or a research laboratory?
- the culture of the organization – 'this is the way that we do things around here'.
- what's being done – a product launch or a routine task?
- how the followers like to be led – 'tell me what to do' or 'can we talk about this?'

This means that there isn't a single unique style of leadership that will always produce the best results. As they say, it all depends. The style of leadership that you'd use in a battlefield situation would be different from the one you'd use in a 'work-a-day' office situation. Your effective leadership will answer the needs of the task in hand and the group working on that task.

'What a man dislikes in his superiors, let him not display in the treatment of his inferiors.'

Tsang Sin, Fifth Century BC

'The true leader is always led.'
Juliana of Norwich, Fourteenth Century

'A leader is a dealer in hope.'
Napoleon I, 1810

'People ask the difference between a leader and a boss . . . The leader works in the open, and the boss in covert. The leader leads, and the boss drives.'

Theodore Roosevelt, 1910

'I believe in benevolent dictatorship – provided I am the dictator.'
Richard Branson, 1984

'Today's successful business leaders will be those who are most flexible of mind.'

Tom Peters, 1987

'The leader's primary role is to act as visionary and motivator.'
Michael Hammer and James Champy, 1993

'The first problem with all of the stuff that's out there about leadership is that we haven't got a clue about what we're talking about.'

Peter Senge, 1999

LISTENING

The way that we do, or don't, listen to what others say to us is one of the things that sorts the goats from the sheep when it comes to surviving in an organization. Good listeners hear, listen to, digest and respond to what people say. Bad listeners hear and retort. The difference between hearing and listening is more than just a matter of words. When you hear something, the outer parts of your ear guide the pressure waves of the sounds in towards the membranes of your inner ear. These vibrate in response to the complex wave patterns of those sounds. These vibrations are then converted, by means of an extraordinarily neat and simple bone mechanism, into nerve impulses which pass to your brain for processing and identification. This process – hearing – is a purely physical reaction to sound waves. It enables you to detect and interpret the sounds that other people are making. But is it listening?

The answer is that it isn't. Hearing and listening are very different and the difference is to do with the ways that you respond to the reflex of hearing. Hearing is passive and involuntary, listening is active. Listening demands the listener's voluntary participation and an investment of time and energy. When you listen you not only acquire, understand and evaluate information, you also get hints and signs about how the speaker is feeling about you or the subject that's being talked about. Not listening – just hearing – means that you miss out on these. Any subsequent decisions and judgements that you make are based on what is the minority of the total 'message'. When you listen, rather than just hear, you acknowledge the speaker and endorse their value to you. How many times have you heard about, or even said of, a bad or busy manager, 'she (or he) doesn't listen to me'.

When you listen you acknowledge, in a very real and tangible way, the value of the speaker and what he or she has to say. The person who only hears is more concerned with his or her own thoughts and rehearsing what she or he intends to say when the speaker has finished. All of this isn't just important to survival in your organization – it's vital. For listening is key to the all-important process of communication (*see* **Communication**).

If you can't see the difference between hearing and listening, try this simple test with a friend or partner. One of you speaks first – briefly and clearly. The other person is only allowed to respond to what has been said

after they've correctly summarized what the first person said. The
Listeners amongst you will get it right – the Hearers won't! When you've done that here are some rules for effective listening:

1 **Indicate by your manner that what is being said is being absorbed:**
   - look, encourage by nodding, and reinforce – 'I see'.

2 **Avoid self/others interrupting:**
   - interrupt only to ask for clarification.

3 **Resist distractions:**
   - listen for the theme of the message;
   - focus on what the speaker is saying;
   - avoid verbal, visual or physical distractions.

4 **Don't judge content or delivery:**
   - concentrate on hearing 'what' is said, not 'how' it is said.

5 **Avoid daydreaming:**
   - don't tune out;
   - force yourself to listen;
   - maintain eye contact, lean forward, occasionally summarize – 'So you are saying . . .'

6 **Let him or her talk:**
   - don't rush to fill the speaker's pauses;
   - if she or he stops, encourage them to continue – 'Go on', or 'What happened then?'

7 **Keep your mind open:**
   - listen in an understanding way;
   - don't prejudge what they will say before they've said it!

8 **Listen between the words:**
   - be alert for omissions, sometimes the essential message is contained in what is not said;
   - listen for feeling as well as meaning;
   - ask yourself is the speaker: critical or neutral, open or evasive, optimistic or pessimistic, confident or defensive, etc.?

9 **Check your interpretation of the speaker's message:**
   - clarify by: 'So the situation is . . .?', or 'Do you mean . . .?';
   - ask questions if you don't understand;
   - ask yourself: 'Do you really know what they are saying?'

LOYALTY

You don't see loyalty around much these days. When you do it's usually in company with other, almost as rare, attributes such as constancy, fidelity and trustworthiness. In the dictionary, loyalty is described as 'faithful adherence to one's promise, oath, word of honour'. You'll use it to describe the way that people (and pets) behave towards one another or other people. It's also used in formal oaths – as when you swear to support the Constitution of the United States – and, sometimes, in marriage vows.

In your organizations, employee loyalty is much talked about. There was a time, of course, when all employees were loyal. This was the sort of loyalty that was given in exchange for jobs-for-life. People who 'did their job' and didn't screw up had the right to expect guaranteed employment for the duration of their working lives. As a result they acted as loyal employees. Nowadays, things are different. The waves of corporate downsizing (*see* **Downsizing**), re-engineering and restructuring have eroded that sort of loyalty to the point where it doesn't exist. The employee of the twenty-first century is seen as – and often encouraged to be – a free agent. As a result people, who in the past would have put the interests of their employers ahead of their own, now act in ways designed to guard their own 'self' interests. Yet there is still a recognition that what's called employee loyalty can – and does – make a substantial contribution to the survival and success of an organization.

So where does this leave loyalty and, more to the point, how does this affect you and your organizational survival rating? The first thing to recognize in finding the answer is that the old sort of loyalty is dead and buried. The second thing is to realize that real loyalty can't be bought – it has to be earned. Its fine detail is negotiated, rather than dictated. It's about mutual respect and tolerance. Why not give it a try?

LUCK

The word 'luck' entered the English language sometime during the fifteenth or sixteenth centuries. Initially a gambling term, its use quickly spread well beyond the race courses and gaming tables, to be used about any event or situation. When you think about it you'll soon see that luck has three basic characteristics:

1 Luck is fickle. It only occurs as a result of chance or accidental events – it can't be created, purchased or manufactured.

2 Luck is binary in nature. It's either 'good' or 'bad'. 'Good' luck occurs when the outcomes of chance events favour you and 'bad' luck occurs when these act against you or your interests.

3 Luck is something that only happens to people. Motor cars cannot be lucky or unlucky – but their drivers can.

So, how can luck help you in your attempts to survive in the organizational jungle? The first step is that you must accept that luck will only attend your efforts when it – rather than you – wants to. Despite the fact that the arrival of 'good luck' is a welcome event you cannot presume upon its presence when you need it. This means that you must make your plans and run your projects on the assumption that while luck might influence their outcomes you cannot rely on it doing so. But this doesn't mean that you should ignore the presence of luck. If you do this, if you turn your back on luck, then you'll leave yourself unable to exploit a fortuitous opportunity or unable to defend against the consequences of unpredictable 'bad' outcomes.

What's needed is a 'tightrope act' – one balanced between blind faith in luck and turning one's back on it. The key lies in your preparation; the more that you prepare yourself to accept, rather than fight, unforeseen events

> *'I am a great believer in luck, and I find the harder I work the more I have of it.'*
> Stephen Leacock

then the more freedom you have to choose the response which is the most appropriate when they occur. The trick is to work hard at that preparation without becoming bound by the outcomes of that work.

At its core the process of management has the act of controlling what other people do. Much has been written about the how and why of this process. But almost all of that august body of work has failed to identify a simple but incredibly important fact about it. That is that this act of management is built upon a false assumption – that those who are managed are not capable of managing themselves.

This assumption is not only wrong, it's also unhealthy. If you doubt that then ask yourself this simple question: How many times have you seen a senior manager in your organization who didn't look careworn and overworked? If your organization is like most organizations then the answer will be that you haven't. But if you're not sure then try another question. Ask yourself how many times have you seen a senior manager in *any* organization who broke into song when he or she felt like it (*see* **Singing**); or laughed spontaneously (*see* **Laughter**); or delayed the business of a meeting to tell a joke (*see* **Meetings**). Your answer will probably be either that you've never seen them happen or if they did happen it was on the day that manager retired.

When you look around at the people in your organization you'll detect the results of all this managing. You'll be able to see where enthusiasm turned into cynicism, openness into self-interest and willingness and flexibility turned into rigidity and a 'not my job' attitude. These sorts of changes are not good. They happen because someone – a manager – assumes that these enthusiastic, open, willing and flexible people can't manage their own efforts. Testing that assumption is easy. Think about the people in a group that you're familiar with and ask yourself what they do outside work. You'll probably find that they do all sorts of things that are creative and involve management skills. They'll tell you – by what they do outside work – what they could do inside work – if only the organization would let them.

MANAGEMENT CONSULTANTS 1

There's a saying that tells you that if you ask a management consultant what the time is then he or she will borrow your watch, give you the answer – and then walk off taking your watch with them! In an ideal world, all management consultants would be like you are – modest, unassuming and well qualified people with a wide experience of a number of industries and the ability to work *with* people to solve their problems. But, of course, they aren't all like that – any more than you are. Management consultants often get a mixed press. Client confidentiality agreements usually mean that you don't get to hear about the really great stuff that they did at the ABZ or the XyG corporation and their work with public bodies means that you do hear about what appear to be their high fee rates.

So what can management consultants give you and how does it help? The best of management consultants can give you a service that's independent; advisory in nature; draws on leading edge professional knowledge and skills; and is capable of providing appropriate and relevant solutions to your organization's problems.

The key words here are independent, advisory, professional, practical and relevant. What the best consultants do is to work *with* the organization's people to identify practical solutions to real problems. When they depart they leave a working solution that's been accepted and taken on board by those people. This means that the organization can plug into the specialist skilled manpower that it needs – but doesn't have. When the job's finished it can bid farewell to all that manpower without the usual severance costs. It also means that an organization can get access to the sort of 'we've done this before' experience that may not be available in its own workforce.

However, there are two things that management consultants certainly are not. The first of these is that they aren't magicians – they don't have a brief case full of miracle solutions. If they try to tell you that they have — then beware! (*see* **Management Consultants 2**). The second thing is that they aren't infallible. After all, they are human and humans do make mistakes. So make sure that you've got a penalty clause in your contract with them.

MANAGEMENT CONSULTANTS 2

Like the rest of us, management consultants have faults. Here are some examples:

The number crunching consultants

This sort of consultant is obsessed with numbers and will spend ages analysing and correlating facts and figures about your particular and current problem. After many months and spending a pile of your money, the best that they will tell you is that the situation is worse than you thought it was. The worst that she or he will come up with is to tell you that while your original intuition – about something being wrong – was correct, they can't quite put their finger on what it is. They then go, leaving you confused, with less money and the original problem still to solve.

The technological wizard consultants

The latest, the newest and the brightest technology is this sort of consultant's 'fix' and you, the client, are merely an enabling mechanism towards his or her exploration of that technology. Whether that technology is relevant to your organization or even developed to the point where it can be used outside the research lab is often beside the point. This sort of consultant often leaves the client with a pile of high-tech equipment whose value has just dropped through the floor and needs a PhD in particle physics to keep it operational. The problem has, however, changed from 'how do we do it better?' to 'how do we get back to where we were before?'

The 'we can see inside their heads' consultants

This sort of consultant's claim to fame lies in his or her knowledge of the latest academic theories about what makes people tick. Since most of these were developed from lab work on rats or college students in the mid-west of North America, applying them often involves a huge leap in the dark. This is a leap that you, not the consultant, will be taking. Beware of the more extreme versions of this stuff and make sure you've got escape or penalty clauses in your contract.

HOW NOT TO No. 6: THE PLAN
A Cautionary Tale

In the Beginning there was a Plan. This Plan was created by Beings from another Plane of Existence – who were called Consultants. These Consultants had laboured much in the Furnace of Bright Ideas and Creativity and, from the dross of Assumptions, had moulded a Plan. And this Plan, which was full of Promise and Forward Thinking, was given to those on this Plane of Existence with much Pomp and Blowing of Trumpets. When the Workers heard about this Plan, Hope sprang into their Hearts for they had been downtrodden and long suffering.

But when these Workers looked at the Plan, they started to wail and beat their breasts and to cry out loud saying: 'This will not work – it is foolish.' And their masters, who were called Supervisors, said to them: 'Why do you cry so – What is it that causes you to lament and weep?' And the Workers said: 'The Assumptions, the Assumptions – they are false, utterly false and the Plan is a Crock of Faeces and Stinketh.' So the Supervisors went to their Managers and said: 'Our Workers have seen The Plan and they tell us that its Assumptions are False. They say This Plan is a Bucket of Dung and its smell is Vile.' So the Managers went to their Section Heads and said to them: 'The Plan is seen by the Workers to be a Container of Excrement which is so strong that none can stand by it.' After much thought, the Section Heads, who were wise and strong, said to each other: 'We must speak about this with our Elder brothers, The Division Heads.' And they told their Elder brothers that: 'We have heard that the Workers have said that The Plan is a Hollow Vessel which is full of Fertilizer and none can abide its strength.' And the Division heads came together. There was much gnashing of teeth and wailing for they knew that the Plan had been the child of He who Rules from on High and is called the Chief Executive Officer. So the Division Heads said: 'We must tell our Fathers, The Directors.' And so with eyes cast down and with trembling voices they sought and were granted audience with The Directors. At that audience the Division Heads said: 'We have heard that it is said that The Plan contains that which aids plant growth and is very strong.' And the Directors looked upon them and said: 'You have done well, my children, to tell us this and we will carry the message to He who Rules from on High and is called the Chief Executive Officer.' And the Directors carried this message to He who Rules from on High and said to him: 'The Plan is said to Promote Growth and to be very Powerful.'

So He who Rules from on High and is called the Chief Executive Officer smiled and said: 'We must tell our Friends the Shareholders of this Good

News.' So He rose to his feet and blew the Golden Trumpet which was called Public Relations and summoned the Shareholders to A Great Meeting. And at this Meeting He who is called the Chief Executive Officer said: 'My friends, I have Good News for you for my children have seen my Plan and have told me that it is a Powerful Plan which will actively promote Growth.' And the Shareholders stood and cheered for they loved He who Rules from on High and is called the Chief Executive Officer for he had given them much profit. And so it came to be that the Plan was called Good and Policy and it was implemented. But when the Workers heard that this was so they began to be angry and to talk amongst themselves, saying: 'We have not been listened to, they nod and smile when we speak – but they do not listen. We must make them listen!' And those amongst them who were grey haired said: 'My Brothers, we have seen before that those who Supervise and Manage us are but as clever children with no wisdom or experience. We must be kind to these children and show them that the MBAs and the Diplomas which they smite us with are but as dust before the Wisdom of Experience.' And so the Workers took those Assumptions which had been used to create the Plan and exposed them to the twin Suns of Pragmatism and Reality and lo – they shrivelled and dried and became as dust before their eyes. And the old, grey haired, and wise workers took this dust to their Supervisors and showed them that the Plan was built on dust and sand. And the Supervisors said: 'Oh woe – we are all up that creek that stinketh and none of us have a paddle.' And the grey haired, wise and old workers said: 'Fear not, our brothers, for all of us together can overcome this problem and make it so that we all will rejoice and that He who is called the Chief Executive Officer will be pleased and happy. This we can do by the dance that our Mothers and Fathers taught us all when we were young and that we have forgotten as we grew older.' And the old grey haired workers showed the dance to both their Worker Brothers and their Management Brothers and told them its name which was the Dance of Communication. And lo as they all danced together the Assumptions began to change and became strong and full of truth. And from on high there came those Beings from another Plane, the Consultants, and they too joined in the Dance which is called Communication. And lo the Plan too began to change and grow and shine as a beacon to all around. So began the times that are now called the Times of Growth and Expansion and those Times went on for many years. After a while, however, they all forgot the stink of the false assumptions and the Dance which is called Communication began to get slower and the Times of Growth and Expansion come to an end – but that is another story for another time.

MEETINGS

Meetings are rather like family weddings or funerals – you don't really want to go, but you feel annoyed if you're left out. This is just one of the reasons why you get involved in so many meetings. It's estimated that in the United States alone some *11 million* meetings take place *every day*. These meetings take place over breakfast, lunch and dinner and any time in between. They take up enormous amounts of time and generate almost as much paperwork.

These meetings fall into one of three groups:

- bad meetings;
- unnecessary meetings; and
- good meetings.

Bad meetings are, unfortunately, in the majority. They are bad because they:

- last too long;
- try to do too much;
- involve too many people;
- are poorly planned;
- aren't prepared for;
- are badly chaired;
- involve people who: don't want to be there, or don't want to take decisions, or haven't got any authority to take decisions.

Unnecessary meetings are the next biggest group. They:

- don't have a clear cut, commonly understood purpose;
- happen at the wrong time;
- involve either too many people or the wrong people;
- are held because it's routine or traditional;
- could be replaced by other ways of communicating.

The third and final group – the Good meetings – are rare, precious and don't happen very often. When they do they:

- have a purpose that's clearly understood by everybody who attends;
- have an agenda focused towards achieving that purpose;

- are only attended by a limited number of people who are prepared, need to be there and can contribute;
- have a chairperson who: sticks to the agenda, ensures the meeting doesn't waste time, and summarizes.

But even an ideal chairperson needs effective meeting members. Having the skills to be one will make a major contribution to your survival rating. If you're going to be an effective meeting member then you'll need to be able to:

- speak clearly and concisely;
- listen actively;
- negotiate and compromise;
- cope with stress yet avoid destructive conflict;
- demonstrate independent judgement;
- be creative and innovative;
- carry out tasks and assignments resulting from the meeting with thoroughness and vigour.

'I've called this meeting to set a date for the meeting to agree the agenda for the annual general meeting.'

MIND AND BODY

If you could take the top off your head and see into your mind what you'd see would be a state of constant commotion. You are constantly thinking about this or that, turning this or that problem over, deciding what to do – or not to do. If you think of your mind as a pool of water then, most of the time, it's pretty stirred up and muddy. In this state you can't find the time or space to get a handle on where you are or what is happening to you. But if you let it be, let the muddy waters clear, then you'll gradually become more relaxed and less stressed. One way of doing that is to use the process of meditation.

Meditation has been around for a long time – particularly in the cultures of Tibet, India and South Eastern Asia. Now, its value is beginning to be understood in the West. It's becoming common to find meditation used in all sorts of organizations. People meditate before corporate creativity sessions, during coffee breaks, before and after work and prior to tests – in fact, anywhere that they need to. Its aim, in these and many other situations, is to relax and de-stress you. But that's not all it can do for you. For it can also put you in touch with a very subtle level of consciousness – one that we all possess but usually ignore – and enable you to use that to handle stress, be creative and focus your energy effectively. All of which will help your survival rating.

So how do you meditate? The first thing to realize is that meditation isn't a particular way of sitting or breathing; it is a state of mind. This means that you can do it while you are walking, cooking, working, riding on a bike or just sitting. But it's not about striving towards that state of mind, it's about simply being – learning to let yourself be as you are rather than thinking in a particular way. Most of us, however, need to learn how to meditate by sitting before we can transfer it into our everyday activities. This will take time. You'll have to sit a lot and learn how to relax; you'll have to forget about striving to be the perfect meditator (*see* **Relaxez-Vous**). The easiest and best way to learn about sitting meditation is to:

■ learn and establish a good basic sitting practice by attending classes at your local meditation centre; and

■ meditate, meditate and meditate.

Here's a good method to start with:

- Sit, comfortably, either in a chair or cross-legged on a cushion but with a straight back.
- Settle your mind and body; relax.
- Check up on your thoughts – why do you want to meditate, and what do you want to achieve?
- Spend some time concentrating on your breath.
- Breathe naturally.
- Focus on the feeling as your breath enters and leaves your body.
- Count your breaths in groups of five or ten. If you lose count or your mind wanders, start again.
- Be content to stay in the present. Accept whatever thoughts come and go without judgement.
- At the end of your meditation spend a moment dedicating the positive energy that you've generated towards the objective or subject of your meditation.

It's a good idea to meditate every day for fifteen to twenty minutes. When you do that remember to:

- give to yourself the time and space that you need;
- be disciplined enough to keep your mind and body together in one place;
- be patient with yourself;
- persevere in the way you overcome your laziness;
- focus yourself and be alert during your meditation;
- accept, without judgement, the thoughts that pass through your mind.

MIRACLES

It seems to be in the nature of things that miracles don't happen very often. They are those infrequent and outside-your-ordinary-experience events the like of which you've never heard of or experienced before. When one of these happens and there isn't a rational explanation for it then the label 'miracle' gets attached. This serves two purposes. First, it enables you to classify – and hence confine – the unexplainable. And second, it reminds you of the positive nature of the event. For there are no negative miracles – they are all positive, life-enhancing, events. But they are also events that lack explanation or evident cause. This seems to encourage you to believe that they, or something similar, might just happen again.

But are miracles really as unpredictable as that? The *Oxford English Dictionary* says that a miracle, at least in its non-religious form, is a 'remarkable development in some specified area'. If you think about this definition you'll soon find that it gives some hope that the occurrence of these events is susceptible to influence. You can begin to hope, for example, that the amazing events that occur when a group of people is transformed into a team of co-workers – with the resultant leap in creativity, communications and achievements – can be duplicated or even re-created (*see* **Teams**). For these and other similar events are the miracles of our organizations. They may be buried or hidden in the routines of our work-a-day lives but they are 'remarkable developments'. They are the 2 + 2 = 5 (or even 7) events and they always involve people. Indeed, without people these miracles could not come into being. But they also need those who manage those people to believe that, given enough support and trust, they will 'walk on water' and do that when least expected. Make sure that you have enough space to create your own 'miracles' and to do so each and every day.

Retrospective vision is always 20/20. When you look back at the past you can see that some of the things that you've done turned out to be mistakes. These mistakes, which time and others reveal to you, will have occurred for a number of reasons. They may, for example, have happened because you misheard or misunderstood what was said to you or because you misinterpreted or failed to understand what you read. They may also have happened because you forgot what you were supposed to do or because of an error in judgement on your part. There are very, very few of us who do not make mistakes. So, given that this is so, why is it that there are so few of us who, on recalling our past mistakes, do not experience a shudder of embarrassment or even guilt about them?

The answer lies in the nature of the relationship that you have with your mistakes. Most of you are unwilling to accept or acknowledge your mistakes. You avoid them. You evade coming face to face with them. As a result, you miss out

> 'The man who makes no mistakes does not usually make anything.'
>
> William Connor Magee

on the opportunity to learn from them. Doing this – acknowledging your mistakes and learning from them – is an act of both courage and growth. It's also one that will increase your survival rating. What stops you doing it is fear – fear of getting it wrong and being seen to do so by those with whom you work. In some workplaces, making a mistake leads to scorn, derision or even punishment, irrespective of the magnitude or the consequences of the mistake. This, inevitably, leads to a 'culture' in which mistakes are covered up and hidden – rather than acknowledged and owned; a culture in which blame and punishment are the norms – rather than support, constructive examination and learning (*see* **Archaeology – Corporate**; **Norms**; **Freaks – Control and Other**).

Yet a mistake can be a gift – one that you can give to yourself. It can be an opportunity for you to learn, not only about yourself but also about others. But that's not all that it has for you, for it also gives you a chance to avoid making the same mistake another time. When you turn this gift aside, reject it, then you increase, by several orders of magnitude, the probability of repeating the same mistake – and that doesn't seem a sensible thing to do, does it?

MOANING

Moaning is one of those things, like getting married or staying in bed until lunchtime, that most of you do from time to time. But, unlike those other self-indulgences, moaning is usually thought of in a negative way. A moaner is a complainer, a murmurer, a pessimist.

But nothing could be further from the truth. For when you moan you express your desire for things to improve and your hope that things will get better. You want the weather to improve, the trains to run on time and politicians to actually do what they said they would do. All of these wishes and hopes are perfectly reasonable expressions of the human condition. Not moaning means accepting the inevitable, allowing the Great Steam-Roller of Life to run over you. The way things are in organizations it's not surprising that most of your moaning is about what happens in there. You moan about bosses who don't listen to you (*see* **Bosses – Not So Good**), the systems that don't allow you to answer your customers' needs (*see* **Adaptability**), the promises that get broken (*see* **Promises**) and the stupid games that get played (*see* **Games**; **Pecking Order**; **Dominance**). But, like most things, moaning comes in two varieties: bad moaning and good moaning.

Good moaning is constructive, focused, clear and understandable. It's also one of the first signs that the catalyst of change is at work. When you moan well you express your individuality in very real and concrete terms; you put claim to your right to complain. Good moans come from well-intentioned loyal employees who are trying to do their best to make the organization a better one. Moaning well and, just as importantly, responding constructively to it, is what sorts the sheep from the goats.

Bad moaning is just the opposite. It's destructive, diffuse, unfocused and *boring*. It's almost as bad – and as dangerous – as those strange practices that go on in some organizations and involve employees in singing songs about how good the company is (*see* **Bull**). Bad moaning does little to help organizations change for the better; quite the contrary. It bungs up communication channels and reinforces stereotypes. In the end, it's up to you which sort of moaning – good or bad – that you indulge in. Try to remember that while good moaning can be seen as being self-indulgent, it *can* and often *does* lead to constructive change. But bad moaning can only be self-destructive.

MONOLOGUES AND CHATS

Sometimes when we talk to each other the things that we say are brief and limited. They are the 'Hi's' and 'Hello's' that you exchange when you see someone you know on the way to work or when you pass each other in the corridor on your way to yet another meeting. Circumstances or lack of time dictate that you can't allow the conversation to develop as it might; you are preoccupied with other tasks, problems or targets. Brief as they are, these exchanges are often full of 'coded' questions and comments like 'How are you?' – questions often asked knowing that there isn't time to hear the answer. But there are other verbal exchanges that also fail to reach the high peaks of full communication (*see* **Communication**; **Conversations**; **Dialogues and Discussions**). The Chat and the Monologue are two of these.

The first of these – the chat – occurs you indulge in idle, frivolous talk. But this can have a purpose. For some of chatting is about talking for talking's sake or social grooming – talking about subjects that encourage your 'togetherness'. These sorts of talk often dominate chats. At their worst, chats are ways of avoiding anything but nominal social contact. At their best, they are situations in which we use words to revel in the ambiguities and complexities of our relationships and to explore their boundaries. Chats come naturally to some people and are difficult for others. But chats have the potential to upgrade, extend and expand your relationships; they are the ways in which you talk up – rather than down – to the people with whom you share your workplace.

Monologues, however, are not so easily justified. Typically, a monologue is long and delivered by a single person. At its best, it can be a reflective soliloquy in which the speaker shares his or her inner dialogue with you. At its worst, it is a tirade, a harangue, an avalanche of criticism or judgement. But whatever its style or intent may be, the fact remains that you, as a captive listener, are excluded from active participation in the monologue. As such, it fails to be either effective or communicative. Take care not to be drawn in by its seductions for it will earn you enemies, rather than friends.

NEGOTIATING

You are all negotiators. You learn the language of bargain and barter at your mother's knee and, having done that, you go on to use it for the rest of your lives. You negotiate with everyone – bosses, partners, children, lovers, friends, enemies, co-workers, suppliers, contractors and customers. There are no exclusions, no exemptions from this practice of negotiation. The list of things that you negotiate about is just as encyclopaedic. In your organization you negotiate about things like how much you get paid, how much you pay someone else, who's in charge, or who decides what and when. Some of these negotiations are formal. They involve teams of negotiators – rather than single individuals – and draw on complex sets of written and unwritten rules (*see* **Unwritten Rules**). However, it's informality that's the rule for most of your workplace negotiations. They take place at the coffee machine or the water fountain, over the lunch table or the desk, in the corridor or across the workshop. They are day-to-day, hour-by-hour events; they are about who will do what, when it gets done and, sometimes, why it needs to be done.

Some of you carry out your negotiations well. You get what you want and at a price that's less than you might have been prepared to settle for. However, most of you muddle through your negotiations; you fall into success by accident rather than by design. Even when you achieve that success you often remain unsure as to whether the other side would have given you more or whether you'd given them too much. Changing that, becoming an effective negotiator, is a key contributor to your survival rating.

Here are some points to show you how to achieve that:

■ Recognize that all negotiations:
  – involve people, acting either for themselves or for others;
  – start from a conflict between your needs and those of others;
  – use well established ways of exchanging things, such as bargaining or bartering;
  – are almost always face-to-face – drawing strongly on your words, gestures and facial expressions;
  – are all about the future, rather than the past;
  – reach an endpoint when you and the other side agree.

■ Your chances of being successful in your negotiations will increase when you:
- are clear about what you want to achieve;
- have decided what your best, worst and probable outcomes are;
- can find the common ground between you and the other side;
- go for win–win – rather than win–lose – results.

■ Worthwhile agreements will come when you:
- are patient;
- get your timing right;
- are open to closure from the very beginning of your negotiation;
- respect the other side.

Being able to negotiate well isn't just a workplace skill. It's also a skill that colours, flavours, influences the way you live the rest of your life. It is, to use the jargon of the social psychologists, the ultimate 'transferable' skill. Learn and use it well for it will add benefit to the whole of your life.

'I'm sure we can reach an agreement on this.'

NETWORKING

Networking is cool, networking is the key to survival and success in the organizations of the twenty-first century. People who network:

■ have lots and lots of contacts;

■ have open and informal relationships with them;

■ make sure that their contacts are warm and 'in the loop';

■ work hard to ensure that that these contacts are mutually beneficial;

■ keep on adding to these contacts.

Some people have a natural talent for networking. They're the ones who – when you ask them if they know about something or other – say 'No – but I know a woman (or man) who does.' The contacts that they have are extensive and valuable. They extend well beyond the formal boundaries of any single organization and they open doors. They are about give-and-take, caring, friendship, mutual trust and need (*see* **Caring**). Organizations don't like networks. This is because:

■ they breach the fire wall that's designed to protect the secrets of the organization (*see* **Secrets**);

■ they bypass and overtake the formal communications networks of the organization – every time; and

■ your personal network is outside their control.

So what can a network do for your survival and how do you build one? A good personal network – one that works – is rather like a kind of capital account. It's there for you to draw on when times are hard and to invest in when times are good. But – unlike most bank accounts – it's also there for others to draw on and invest in. An account like this can't help but be a good thing for your survival. It will be there when times are hard (*see* **Downsizing; We're Going To Have To Let You Go**) and it'll be there when you need to turn your hoped-for future into a reality (*see* **Your Future**). Building a network takes time, patience and a willingness to give people access to your knowledge and contacts. It also helps if you like people!

NEW

Most of you are fascinated by things that are new. After all, the glitter and gloss of the new is far more attractive and intriguing than the dents, scratches and familiarity of the old. As a result, your relationship with the new often starts off on the wrong foot. It starts with a leap in the dark that's premature and unplanned. It's a leap that leaves behind an old that still has value for us. This state of affairs is at its most obvious when you look at the way that you change the computers. There's always a bigger or faster one that's just come onto the market. But it's also true of your relationship with ideas about the workplace. Concepts such as Scientific Management, Theory X/Theory Y, T Groups, Management by Objectives, Brainstorming, Management Grid, Decision Trees, Zero Base Budgeting, Strategic Business Units, Value Chains, Quality Circles, MBWA, Matrix Organizations, Just In Time, Optimized Production Technology, Total Quality Management and Re-engineering have all, at some time, been new. They had their time and then passed into obscurity, often having failed to produce the results they promised. Failure rates as high as 70 to 80 per cent have been reported. But what seems to be emerging

> 'New roads: new ruts.'
> G.K. Chesterton

now is an understanding that *new* doesn't necessarily equal *best* – or even *good*. What's raising its head is the truth that a knee-jerk response to the newest fad in the lexicon of management ideology can be positively harmful to an organization.

Surviving these ideological hurricanes is always challenging and often difficult. But it can be worthwhile, and it's *that* potential that can lead you to take the risk, to leap into the dark. But if you're going to turn a 70 per cent failure rate into a 100 per cent success rate for this leap then you need to do things differently. Here are some ideas for you to try:

- Use trials and listen to what people say.
- Learn from your mistakes (*see* **Mistakes**).
- Sell your ideas to everybody – not just your boss (*see* **Change**).
- Work hard to get commitment.
- Don't throw the baby out with the bathwater.

NORMS

In its original form, the word norm – as 'norma' – meant a square used by carpenters or masons. This later changed to mean a standard, a pattern or a rule. It's this version that's used in our organizations to describe the ways that we *ought* to behave. So when you look at the norms in your organization you'll see that, at their core, they are all about acceptable ways of behaving. They are ways of doing things that are approved of and admired by that organization. When you behave in those ways – or conform to those norms – it generates the sort of organizational togetherness that tells you 'all's well'. The pressure to meet these norms can be considerable. When you don't meet them, all sorts of persuasion, pressure and sanctions (*see* **Persuasion**, **Dominance**; **Bullying**) can be applied to make you 'toe the line'. If these fail, then the ultimate sanction is applied – that of ejection from the organization (*see* **We're Going To Have To Let You Go**). The one exception to all of this occurs when a non-conforming person is given a 'license to be different' because of their particular and unique set of skills and abilities or their contributions to the organization. This situation is very rare. Even when it does happen, it provides no guarantee of the organization's continuing acceptance of non-conformity (*see* **Eccentricity**).

All social groups develop norms and often fiercely protect them. But that doesn't mean that you have to accept them unconditionally. For they are often about protecting the status quo and hence about ensuring the survival, continuity and stability of the old. As such they are about resisting, rather than embracing, change. They act in ways which increase the rigidity and inflexibility of the organization (*see* **Change**). All of this does little to help you to survive your organization. It rejects, for example, adaptability (*see* **Adaptability**) and turns aside from creating the sort of customer relations that are based on value – rather than utility (*see* **Customers**). But challenging the old norms of your organization – and turning them into new, more flexible, norms – isn't an easy task. It demands skill, grit and determination. Perhaps the organizations of the future will only have one norm – that of having no norms.

NOSE TO NOSE

The organization is one of those places – like 'planes, trains or public buildings – where you have little choice about who you spend your time with. You rarely get to choose the people you work with and yet you spend as much, if not more, time with them as you do with your partners, families or friends. These people include your co-workers, your bosses (*see* **Bosses – Good**; **New**; **Not So Good**; **Terrible**) and your acquaintances. Some of these you'll count as friends and others you won't (*see* **Friends**). All of this enforced 'togetherness' has its risks – the risk of 'not-getting-on', of incompatibility and, above all, the risk of 'nose-to-nose' conflict. But these aren't the only reasons why you might find yourself in conflict with someone. For you may like each other, get on well together and yet still find yourselves disagreeing about a topic, issue or a decision.

At the core of all conflict situations there lies a single common factor. That is that you find yourself in conflict with someone when the actions of one of you frustrates or limits what the other can achieve. This happens a lot in organizations and, when it does, it shows itself in all sorts of ways. Strong feelings are experienced – people shout, make expansive or dramatic gestures and frown or scowl at each other. While physical violence is rarely present in our organizational conflicts, we can act in ways that disrupt or limit 'normal' communications or result in the withdrawal of co-operation.

There are, essentially, two views about how to deal with this conflict. The traditional view tells us that conflict is 'bad'; it's disruptive, threatening and anti-social. This view says that conflict should be suppressed or, when that's not possible, managed in ways that limit its effects on the organization. The other, more realistic, view accepts that conflict is present in all organizations. As such it is here to stay. This view says that conflict can have 'good' outcomes – such as encouraging consideration of new ways of doing things or causing problems to be brought out into the open and hence solved. This is a view that accepts the fact that organizations are the arenas in which we all strive to satisfy our individual needs and desires.

The choice that you face, on your path to organizational survival, is whether you try to avoid this inevitable conflict or whether you embrace it and find ways of turning it to your advantage. Embracing conflict is a significant step – one that needs skill and courage. But once you've done it you'll find yourself rapidly shifting away from the 'good' versus 'bad' polarity of the traditional view. Then you'll become interested in questions like: How can conflict be made to generate outcomes that benefit the individuals involved and the organization as a whole?; or, At what level does conflict become counterproductive?

Accepting the everyday reality of conflict and using it in ways that achieve constructive and creative outcomes – that satisfy all involved – demands real skill. It's also much more fun than boarding up your doors and windows in a vain attempt to keep out the inevitable conflict. To find the positive side of conflict you need to be able to:

■ keep your 'cool';

■ communicate – in a focused and skilful way (*see* **Communication**);

■ be assertive rather than aggressive (*see* **Assertion**);

■ show that you understand the other person's point of view (*see* **Listening**);

■ generate solutions that both sides agree to (*see* **Negotiating**).

'I'm sure there's a positive side to this conflict.'

OFFICE POLITICS

Working – and surviving – in an organization demands skills. But these aren't just the skills that enable you to do the ABC of your job, the skills of professional competence. For if you're going to survive you also need to develop and use another, just as important, set of skills – the skills of playing politics.

Politics are often thought of as being underhand or devious. The phrase 'office politics' is usually used with disdain, to describe something that's clandestine and furtive. But the politics-free organization doesn't exist. They all contain and sometimes encourage environments in which debate occurs and unanimous agreement is rare. As a result we get politics – or put another way – the art of trying to accomplish things within an organization. This sort of politics is, whether

> 'Politics is the art of the possible.'
>
> R.A. Butler

you like it or not, woven onto the warp and weft of your working life. It's about actions – the sort that you want others to do – and differences – the differences between you and other people that either stop or help these actions taking place.

Here are some tips to help you to get better at your office politics:

- Getting things done means using what power and influence you've got (*see* **Influence – or Power?**).
- Your rank, role or job title isn't as important as the influence you have.
- Using the grapevine and doing that well is key to your office politics (*see* **Grapevines**).
- Don't just ask for people's opinions – get out there and change them.
- Remember that everybody, but everybody, expects to be paid back.
- Win or lose this time, the words 'thank you' will help you to get you a win next time.
- When you get a success, share the credit.
- Remember that good politics make people feel good, bad politics make them angry.

OFFICE ROMANCES

Romance happens everywhere and to almost everyone. It happens when we become attracted to each other and when we fall in love (or lust) with one other. Romance is illogical. It happens despite our best intentions or our current marital status and when it does happen it's impulsive, passionate, emotional and often overwhelming.

But what about romance and the organization? When you think about it you'll soon realize that it would amazing if romance *didn't* appear in our organizations. After all, they're full of people, all working together and sharing interests and commitments. But when that happens, when office romance blooms, what do our employers do? The answer is that most of them don't approve. The main reason for this is that romance is about emotion and emotion is not welcome in the workplace. After all, our employers argue, emotion can lead to irrational behaviour and unpredictability and these can lead to reduced efficiency. This anti-romance stuff can be written into your contract of employment – as when work relationships are forbidden – or one of the unwritten rules of your organization (*see* **Unwritten Rules**). Either way, the result is the same – office romances are a *no-no*. But is this fair or even reasonable? The sad fact is that office romances can make a difference. People do get promoted or given special treatment because they're in a relationship with their boss. When an office romance ends the fall-out can cause havoc in a previously well-ordered and efficient work group. In the UK, employment tribunals regularly hear cases about people who were dismissed, demoted or moved when their 'special relationship' – with the boss – ended. In the USA there are moves, by employers, to limit this fall-out by asking office couples to sign statements declaring that their office romances are voluntary. But not all office romances turn out badly – there are people who fall in love, get married, have children and live happily ever after – all as a result of a chance meeting over the photocopier! But be warned, for romance can strike without warning and, when it does, things will never be the same again.

Organizations, in one form or another, loom over all of our lives. They register your birth and they certificate your death. In between, these organizations are everywhere. They license your marriage, sell you goods or services, educate your children, clean and police your street, permit your driving, provide the television programmes that you watch, print the newspapers, magazines and books that you read, organize and conduct the religious services or political meetings that you attend and provide you with the means to earn the money that you need. In short, they embrace each and every aspect of your life. Your relationship with them can be external – as when you buy the goods or services that they produce – or internal – as when you become a member of an organization.

All of these organizations – irrespective of their size or history – have a 'genetic' code. It's a set of rules, principles and procedures that run through all of their activities in the same way that the DNA code runs through our bodies. This code can be hidden (*see* **Unwritten Rules**), out in the open, new (*see* **New**) or old (*see* **Archaeology – Corporate**). But it's always there. It's this code that creates most of

> '. . . *organizations are in essence socially constructed realities that rest as much in the heads and minds of their members as they do in concrete sets of rules and relations.*'
>
> Gareth Morgan

the problems that you have with your organization. For through it that organization will seek to control, dominate, limit and manipulate you.

The organization that really dominates your life is the one that you work for. This organization monopolizes your waking hours. Its working hours, objectives, procedures, rules and regulations ordain the when, what, where and how of your workplace activities. These you carry out as either full-time 'on-the-payroll' member of staff or as part-time or contract employee. For some of you – a shrinking minority – this organization provides a passport to security, reputation, recognition, self-fulfilment and sometimes wealth. But, for most of you, work is a four letter word, something that you *have* to do in order to get the money to get on with the rest of your life. So why do you – the disenchanted majority – join these organizations? If you asked the man or woman in the street this question you'd get as many answers as questions asked. But beneath the surface of all the answers given would lie common cause. That is that we all join these organizations in order to achieve those goals that we think we are unable to achieve on our own.

But what are those goals? What is it that you and I want to achieve in our working lives – or rather, to be more precise, what is it that we desire to achieve in our lives – working or not? The sad truth is that most of you work to live rather than live to work. You do that in organizations that you don't like and with people that you haven't chosen to work with. You put up with that mostly because you need the money but also because you hope that it might change for the better. But it's also true that most of the organizations that you work for don't like you – they put up with you and your funny idiosyncratic ways because they want something – time, skill, creativity – that you can provide. This is a situation that's not just unsatisfactory – it's also unfulfilling and wasteful.

So, given that this is a state of affairs that's unlikely to disappear overnight, what can you do? Here are some ideas that might help you find your own answer to that question:

- Ask yourself if what you're doing at work is what you *really* want to do.
- If it isn't, ask why, and get a straight answer. Then do something about it!
- Audit your life skills and experience; make sure you include them all, particularly the ones you use outside work.
- Generate a wish-list of things that you'd like to do before you die.
- Check out how the results of your life skills audit can help you achieve this wish-list.
- Next time you come up against one of those life-changing events – like the kids leaving home, getting divorced, being laid off or made redundant – ask yourself this question: 'Is this the time for me to set up my own business?'
- Look at the results of your life skills audit and find the bits that you aren't using at work.
- Find or create work situations where you can use these.
- Find a way to make work more fun.
- Laugh – on the way to work, when you get there and, of course, when you're leaving. After all, you've survived yet another day!
- Build bridges with your co-workers. You'll be surprised what you've got in common.

- Don't forget to include the boss in your bridge-building. You may even get to like him or her.
- Tell someone a joke once a week – but please remember to make it a different one.
- Say thank you to your partner – for their support.

ORGANIZATION CHECKLIST

Great, even good, organizations are seen to behave towards the people who work for them in certain ways. Here are some of them. Add to the list if you need to and then check out your organization against them:

■	Truthful	Yes	☐	No	☐
■	Accountable	Yes	☐	No	☐
■	Disciplined	Yes	☐	No	☐
■	Tolerant	Yes	☐	No	☐
■	Open	Yes	☐	No	☐
■	Answerable	Yes	☐	No	☐
■	Nourishing	Yes	☐	No	☐
■	Respectful	Yes	☐	No	☐
	Total scores:	Yes	☐	No	☐

Makes you think, don't it!

PECKING ORDER

The phrase 'pecking order' was first used to describe the ways that hens behave. Apart from pecking for food, clucking and laying eggs, hens also indulge in what is called 'social behaviour'. They have status and rank, 'in-group' and 'out-group' behaviour (*see* **You're In – or You're Out**) and they compete for food and shelter. The rank of a hen is influenced by a number of factors such as size and aggression. The higher a hen is on the 'pecking order' the more response-free attacks it can get away with. But pecked hens also need to confirm their status and do this by pecking at hens who are below them in the pecking order. This pecking order was quickly seen to be a behaviour pattern which also exists in other groups of social animals – including humans.

But what light does this throw on the ways in which you behave in your organization? The answer lies in the fact that we humans – as social animals – also behave towards each other in ways that are concerned with status, 'in-groups' and 'out-groups', competition, hostility and intimacy (*see* **Competition**; **Dominance**; **You're In – or You're Out**). In groups of people, the 'pecking order' defines things like who speaks, how much they say and the manner they say it. In organizations, things such as job title, office size and car parking space tell you who's what and where on the pecking order. But human pecking orders are rarely established by open combat. More often they are arrived at by hidden conflicts which are political in nature and in which the weapons used are words rather than tooth or claw (*see* **Nose to Nose**; **Office Politics**; **Influence – or Power?**). But the level of violence can still be considerable and many a blossoming career has been cut short because of the knee-jerk defensive reflexes of some ageing senior executive.

However, membership of a pecking order is not mandatory – nobody said you have to behave like a hen and you can help, rather than peck, those below you in the organizational hierarchy. Better still, ask yourself why bother to have a hierarchy? Take a look at **Adaptability**; **Empowerment**; **Freaks – Control and Other**; **Knowledge Worker** to see if they help you find an answer.

PEOPLE

Let's start with the obvious – that is that, just in case you hadn't noticed, people are everywhere. It's also just as obvious – but often forgotten or overlooked – that people are incredibly complicated. Don't let anyone kid you on this one. There's no easy way to understand the ways of the human heart. There are, however, mountains of books, videos and tapes that will try to tell you that they alone have the key to understanding human behaviour. Some of the ideas behind these will be currently popular in your organization while others will have been tried, discarded or rejected. Understanding all of them will present you with a task of such gigantic proportions that 'impossible' is an adjectival understatement.

Nevertheless, taking on board as much of this people stuff as you can manage is worthwhile – it'll increase your survival rating. But doing it well and comprehensively will take a long time – perhaps even a lifetime. What usually happens, on your road to greater understanding of the human species, is that you stumble through a process that goes something like this:

1   You decide – for one reason or another – that you need to know more about 'what makes people tick'. The fact that people don't 'tick' – they actually hum, moan, mutter, sing or shout – doesn't make any difference and certainly doesn't stop or divert you.

2   You then go on courses or root around the mountains of books, tapes and videos – all of which claim to have the answer to your need – looking at each idea in turn and picking up bits from each of them as you go along.

3   You continue to do this until you find one theory or idea that's a 'good-enough' fit with your needs and prejudices (*see* **Prejudice**) to keep you happy for the time being and can accommodate most of the rag-bag of bits that you've picked up on your journey.

4   Then you stop looking.

This process – which is called 'satisficing' (yet another theory!) – usually gets you to the point where you feel you've acquired a pragmatic and workable 'theory' about what makes people do the things that they do. You may even feel that this 'theory' of yours is *so* good that other people need to know about it. You then set yourself up as a consultant (*see* **Management Consultants 1** and **2**). If you're very lucky – and most of us aren't – this 'theory' will keep you happily prejudiced for the rest of your life (*see* **Luck**). But what usually happens is that life comes along and gives you a set of experiences that don't fit your 'theory'. Having tried to force-fit the experience to the theory – which usually doesn't work – you then start the process described above all over again. But this time you take into account what you've learned since your last search. That is to say you learn from your experiences.

Now learning, as you've read elsewhere (*see* **Training**), is good. It helps you to survive in your organization, it helps you adapt what you do and the way that you do it. It helps you cope with, adapt to, even exploit, the waves of change that are endemic to all our lives (*see* **Change**). But when your 'people' theory is too rigid or too doctrinaire then it does just the opposite. It lessens your ability to adapt and change and hence reduces the likelihood of your survival in your organization. What you need is a theory that – like you – is capable of change. The phrase a 'working hypothesis' is a useful one here. Your 'working hypothesis' about people should work – as well as being be flexible, open, caring and careful (*see* **Adaptability**; **Caring**). For as the old saying goes 'There's now't so queer as folk'.

Understanding what made his workers tick perplexed Brian.

HOW NOT TO No. 7: CUSTOMER CARE

By the time John got to the airport it felt as if he'd been struggling uphill ever since he and his Uncle Joe had left home earlier that morning. What with two large suitcases, 80 year old Joe in a wheelchair and an unhelpful cab driver, getting there hadn't been easy. 'Now' John told himself 'we should get some help.' But he didn't. There was the search to find a luggage trolley, leaving Joe parked by the kerbside, followed by the struggle to get Joe, his wheelchair and the loaded trolley to the check-in counter. By the time they were checked in, John felt exhausted. The airline check-in girl gave him directions to the terminal service counter. He was hoping he'd be able to get Joe on one of those golf buggies for the long walk down to the departure gate. No such luck – the counter wasn't manned. On the way down to the gate John picked up one of those tell-us-if-you've-got-a-complaint leaflets. He told them and posted the leaflet in the box provided.

There was a letter waiting when they got back from their holiday: 'Airport Management Group' the embossed heading said. It started by thanking him for filling in the complaint form. 'So far so good' John thought. He read on:

> We regret that we are unable to agree with your suggestion that we failed to provide an adequate service. If exceptions were made for wheelchairs then people with children and more able bodied older people would be able to demand the same privilege. The cost of providing such a service would far outweigh any benefits to us as an operating company. Thank you for your interest.

'So much for customer service!' John said to himself. He kept the letter though. Not too many years later – after his company's bid to provide a customer-care based airport terminal service had been accepted by the town council – he had the pleasure of sacking the man who had signed it.

PERSUASION

These days it seems as if we're immersed in an unremitting, deluge of persuasion. It comes through adverts, television programmes, radio programmes and newspapers, magazines and books. All of these are trying hard to persuade us to buy or do something or to sign up to this particular set of values or to accept that particular point of view. When this persuasion works we are induced to do a particular something; we are won over to a certain course of action.

But these aren't the only ways and means of persuasion. For you also persuade and are persuaded in your workplace. Getting this persuasion right can make an enormous difference to your survival rating. Almost all of your persuasion takes place on an informal and one-to-one basis and most of the time you'll be aiming to either:

■ confirm or reinforce people's existing attitudes or feelings about something that you think is important, or

■ change their attitudes or feelings about something, or

■ get them to take on board a new set of attitudes or feelings.

The ways you use to do this will reflect your experience of what has – or hasn't – worked in the past, what your relative roles are and how well you know each other. Here are some of the ways that are often used to persuade people:

■ Pledge something – like a reward as in 'I'll see you all right' – or a penalty as in 'I'll have to reduce your overtime'.

> '*People are generally better persuaded by the reasons which they have themselves discovered than by those which have come into the mind of others.*'
>
> Pascal

■ Use information and knowledge – either in positive ways – as in 'keep that up and you'll get promoted' – or in negative ways – as in the infamous 'if you don't stop that you'll go blind'.

■ Precondition them – as when you ask how the wife or husband and kids are before asking someone to change shifts or when we tell her she's got a bonus before asking her to move to the Glasgow or Spokane office.

■ Appeal to their feelings about themselves – as in 'you'll feel better (or worse) if you do (or don't do) this.'

- Attribute higher qualities to those who comply – or lower qualities to those who don't – as in 'a mature person would agree' or 'only a childish person would disagree'.
- Call in debts – real or imagined – as in 'you owe me one'.
- Appeal to their sense of fair play, as in 'it's not right to let them do this'.
- Appeal to their self-esteem, as in 'people will think more of you if you agree' or 'people will think less of you if you disagree'.
- Appeal to their concern or regard for others, as in 'you'll really help us all if you agree'.

However you decide to carry out your persuasion, it'll only get to 'yes' if you recognize and use these, the four Laws of Effective Persuasion:

1 Persuasion is an act of communication. As such it must be a shared two-way process if it's going to be effective.
2 Effective persuasion is a conscious act that respects the autonomy of all involved.
3 Effective persuasion creates a change in attitudes.
4 Effective persuasion is an act that is done *with* someone – rather than *to* them.

Doing your persuading *with* someone rather than *to* them will make a crucial difference both to how you do it and its chances of success. It will enable the person that you're persuading to respond with his or her own persuasive ploys – which could be any of those above – and so persuade you. It's also worth remembering that research tells us that you are most easily persuaded by people that:

- you like, trust or respect (*see* **Friends**; **Trust**);
- have power over you (*see* **Influence – or Power?**);
- have a track record of doing successful 'tit-for-tat' deals in the past (*see* **Negotiating**).

PLANNING

The word 'plan' can mean many things to many people. A plan, for example, can be a scheme for the economic development of a country, a drawing or diagram showing the relative positions of the parts of a building or a large-scale map of a small town drawn with considerable detail. All of these are plans – or to put it another way – they are all designs for the ways that events, actions or objects are to be arranged. As such the plan is an everyday commodity and the act of generating one – or planning – is something that many of you do. When you do this what you create is your plan.

The plan that you create is your attempt to control your future (*see* **Your Future**). As such it can be about the qualifications that you intend to gain, the experience that you intend to acquire and the ambitions that you intend to fulfil. It can also be about what you intend to do today or what you plan to do tomorrow, next week, next month or next year. However – despite all of your best intentions – plans don't always work out in the way that you intend them to. As a result, you will almost certainly have to face a reality that is different – in one way or another – to the one that you had planned.

In your workplace, the plans that you make are often challenged. The need for adaptability, the need to respond to customer needs, the tides of market change or sweeping organizational re-engineering are just some of the things that

> 'Life is what happens to you while you're busy making other plans.'
> John Lennon

might act against your plans. But does this disappointment mean that planning is out-of-date and old-fashioned – to be discarded in favour of today's instant responsiveness aided by ever faster computers?

The answer lies not so much in the act of planning but in the way that you use your plans. For these can be more than just lists of intended future actions. They can be powerful visions of your hoped-for futures; they can stake your claim to immortality. And therein lies the plan's deliverance. For as long as you need to reach out and try to shape and control your future then you will need to use the plan to help you achieve that end. But make sure that your plans are adaptable and flexible. For then – with luck – they might just come true! (*see* **Luck**).

A prejudice, so the dictionary tells us, is a 'judgement formed before due examination or consideration; a premature or hasty judgement; a prejudgement.' When you are prejudiced about somebody or something you reach a conclusion about them that is not based on objective facts. This can happen when you:

■ jump to a conclusion because of a previous experience with a similar person, or

■ see people as stereotypes, rather than individuals, or

■ allow your expectations to overwhelm the truth before you.

There are few, if any, good points about prejudice. It's intolerant and often used to enable you to feel superior towards someone. It leads to discrimination (*see* **Racism**; **Ageism**; **Glass Ceilings**). When you are prejudiced you are also:

■ *unreasonable* because you leap to a judgement that has little or no evidence to support it, and

■ *unjust* because you choose to make adverse distinctions or discriminate between people, and

■ *intolerant* because you reject another's freedom to be different.

Typical and common prejudices involve – quite unreasonably and unjustly – women, homosexuals, Jews, Gypsies, Afro-Caribbeans, Latinos, Catholics, old people, poor people – to name but a few.

To do something about prejudice (including your own) you've got to:

■ recognize it for what it is – a prejudice;

■ choose not to react to it;

■ correct or change it as soon as you can.

Doing all of these – not just once, but every time prejudice rears its ugly head – has its pay-offs. You'll become more tolerant, less judgemental and easier to get on with – all of which rate high in the survival stakes.

PROJECTS

Projects can be about anything. They all start as ideas, ideas that become plans, schemes, work-in-progress and then, finally, realities. But most of our projects aren't massive. They involve the everyday events of our working lives; they are about the what, when, how and with what of those lives. But they can also be about your survival in your organization.

All projects are about change and your survival projects will be about changing your situation – moving from where-you-are-now to where-you-want-to-be. But if those projects are going to be successful they'll need to be planned, managed, monitored and controlled – with care, foresight and effectiveness. Achieving that involves the following steps:

- Identify the outcome that you want from your project.
- Be clear, honest and realistic about that outcome.
- If it's a big project break it down into a series of smaller projects.
- Recognize what actions you need to take to achieve that outcome.
- Break these down into a series of small achievable steps.
- Plan how and when you're going to take those steps.
- Identify the resources that you're going to need – and get them.
- Take the first step, carefully.
- Monitor what's happening; check your progress against your plan.
- Take the following steps – one at a time.
- Continue to monitor what's happening.
- Control your progress; use the feedback from your monitoring to focus your corrections.
- Learn as you go along; use experience to get better.
- Be prepared to adapt, change or modify your plan if things aren't working out the way that you intended – but keep going.
- When you achieve your target outcome, celebrate!
- Review how you did – or didn't – do.
- Decide what your next project is.

We all make promises. Some of these are kept and others aren't. A promise is about a future action – something that you intend to do. When you make a promise you also make a commitment to follow through with an action. But promises are not vague diffuse 'somethings' without focus or purpose – they are specific in their intent and also often in their timing. 'I'll send the cheque tomorrow' is one example. But promises aren't just about doing something – they can also be about *not* doing something or about *stopping* doing something. You may promise not to tell anybody else when someone shares a secret with you (*see* **Secrets**) or you may promise to stop smoking. While most promises are made to others you also make them to yourself. You can promise yourself a good holiday at the end of a long and difficult project or to buy the sports car that you've long desired. These 'self' promises are often to do with your self-esteem – you rarely forget them and you almost always keep them (*see* **Self Stuff**).

But this isn't necessarily true of the promises that you make to others. These can be casual, ill-thought out promises, made with unstated conditions attached. The promise 'I'll call you

> 'A promise made is a debt unpaid.'
> Robert Service

back' is typical of these. It's often made as a sort of social 'knee-jerk' reaction – one that seems to mean not that the promiser *will* call you back but that she or he *might* call you back – if not distracted by other matters and if she or he remembers to do so. This sort of promise can also be made as a way of avoiding talking to somebody or becoming entangled in a difficult or embarrassing conversation. Many promises are made and not kept, often made without intent to complete. As such, they are actions not only of dishonesty but also of disrespect towards others. When you make a promise like this you don't add to either the probity or the quality of your relationships with other people. Neither of these will raise your survival rating. Remember the proverb that says, 'promises made in storms are forgot in calms' and limit your promises to those you can keep.

QUALITY

Much, almost too much, has been written about quality. Most of it tells you that quality isn't – as you thought it was – really about goodness, value, worth or condition. It says that *real* quality is about fitness for purpose or use. This change of view or 'quality revolution' has hit most of our organizations – and passed on, leaving them changed. In some cases, the change has been permanent, creating organizations whose aims have been refocused on real quality. In most cases, however, the change has turned out to be temporary and the old ways have soon crept back – albeit with a different jargon (*see* **Jargon**).

But if you're going to survive in your organization, then you really do need to take on board the basic concepts behind this sort of real quality. These will tell you that real quality is about delighting the customer (*see* **Customers**) and making sure that you can do it in ways that are both consistent and adaptable (*see* **Adaptability**). It will underline the need to be clear about your individual responsibility for quality and the fact that this quality is about fitness for purpose. If you were aiming to do this for a whole organization you would need the ideas of Total Quality Management. These are:

- ■ total – because they're about everything – people, material, information, premises and equipment – that contributes to or influences the final product or service, and
- ■ about real quality – as in 'fitness for purpose', and
- ■ concerned with making quality a core management issue – rather than an 'add-on' extra.

Applying these ideas to yourself isn't so very different. What you need to do is to make sure that your view of your quality is:

- ■ total, in that it covers everything that you do;
- ■ about real quality, rather than cost or value;
- ■ managed, because it's integral to all that you do.

This sort of individualized TQM (*see* **Acronyms***)* will change your view of everything that you do – if you let it. It'll change the way you talk to people (*see* **Conversations**) and it'll change the way you see your relationship with them (*see* **Caring**; **Compassion**; **Customers**). And why shouldn't it? After all, *you* are your own internal customer and your co-workers are your external customers. Getting it right for yourself is a vital link in the chain of actions that leads to you delighting all your customers. But it's important that you get the balance right. Meeting – even exceeding – the expectations of your external customer must come first. If you lose that link – and become myopically 'locked into' your own internal processes – then you run the risk of losing that customer. Your communications with them are key towards preventing that happening (*see* **Communication**; **Conversations**; **Dialogues and Discussions**; **Listening**; **Monologues and Chats**).

'I'm sorry, your certificate is 5 cm too wide.'

QUICK – OR SLOW?

These days, quick – or rather, quicker – seems to be the 'in-thing'. You're expected to do your work more quickly, to make your decisions more speedily, spend less time eating your lunch or drinking your coffee, have shorter meetings and spend less 'on-the-road' time between meetings with clients. You send e-mails instead of letters and have 'chats' instead of discussions. The goods and services you buy and sell are now 'next day' rather than 'maybe-next-week'. To help you to do all this your new car has more mph than your old one and your new computer has more MHz than the one you're about to junk. All of these – and other things too numerous to mention – are the symptoms of an inexorable pressure to shift up a gear and conduct your life faster, quicker than you did before. While this 'go-faster' movement has its good points – such as shorter meetings and quicker delivery of the goods you order – it most certainly has a bad side. For not only is it inexorable, it's also insatiable. It's also based on a false premise – that faster equals better. It creates pressure and stress and takes you beyond the point where these are good for you (*see* **Winding Up and Winding Down**).

So perhaps the time has come for you to take a 'time-out' from all this 'go-faster' stuff – and check it out if you're getting the results that you want. Here's some ideas to give you the time to do just that:

- Check your incoming e-mail folder no more than twice a day.
- Let the phone ring at least four times before you answer it.
- Create style and content masters for your frequently used letters, e-mails and faxes – and use them.
- Have fewer meetings.
- Stop multi-tasking and start doing one thing at a time.
- Learn to delegate skilfully – and do it.
- Stop working late and don't take work home.
- Drop taking responsiblity for the things that you can't control.
- Switch your mobile phone off.
- Put aside two ten-minute periods, one in the morning, the other in the afternoon – and leave them completely clear – to do nothing slowly.

'Quiet' is a word that's often used to describe the absence of sound or noise – something that's a rare commodity in the modern world. But it can also be used to describe freedom from other forms of disturbance and interruption or the freedom from worries, excitement or anxiety. You can say that you feel 'quiet' when you feel calm or at peace with yourself and those around you. But when you look at organizations from these viewpoints you shouldn't be too surprised when you find that few of them can be described as 'quiet'.

The fact that they aren't has much to do with the popularity of open-plan, open-door offices and hot-desking systems. In all of these, your personal space is limited. You can be seen and heard by your co-workers – and they by you. In the open-plan office the trilling of 'phones and the half-heard words of other people's conversations drift into the limited personal space that you have. Your open office door – so beloved by the pundits of 'open' management – allows in the noise of passers-by, encourages the casual and distracting 'how-are-you?' and other unrelated-to-work conversations and enables others to view your workplace. In open-plan hot-desking systems you have to repeat the ritual of re-establishing what limited personal space you have every time you enter the common workspace. All of this is allowed, even encouraged, in the name of communication. The idea seems to be that the less personal space you have – to hide in or retire to – the more you will see and hear each other. What happens then – so the theory says – is that your communications with each other get better. These better communications, it is claimed, lead to enhanced effectiveness. But let's not forget the other benefit of all this openness – that is that it also gives managers and supervisors a better line-of-sight, and hence control, of their staff. Of course, what actually happens is the opposite of what's claimed. We learn or try to cope with all this extra noise and distraction by a simple and straightforward tactic – we ignore it – or try to.

But where do quiet and privacy sit amongst all this openness? Are they no longer needed? The answer is, or at least should be, that quiet and privacy are important. We all need times of quiet and we all need a certain level of privacy. When you don't get these – when the balance between your need for these and needs of management to control you is tipped in favour of control – then what happens is that your stress level rises and you become *less* effective (*see* **Winding Up and Winding Down; Mind and Body**).

If you work in one of these 'unquiet' environments then you need to create or ask for – and get – a refuge. This can be as simple as a partitioned, quieter area available to everyone and where the rule is 'leave me alone'. Having a place like this is important. It's where you can work things out, it's where you can opt out of the need for instant reactivity and be reflective and strategic rather then 'knee-jerk' and tactical. The higher the noise in the work area the more a refuge is needed. Creating and encouraging the use of a refuge is a very real expression of trust on the part of management (*see* **Trust**). But if you can't get your boss to see the need for this then take a good look at your personal work space. You'll almost certainly find that there are some small alterations that you can make – like moving a filing cabinet, a plant or a screen – that will increase your privacy level. If none of this works and your boss is still anti-refuge then you may have to face the fact that you're working in an environment that's too lacking in privacy – and hence stressful – for you (*see* **To Boldly Go**). Accepting that this is the wrong workplace for you isn't an admission of defeat. On the contrary, moving out of it is a conscious choice aimed at reducing your stress level and hence increasing your effectiveness and improving your health.

'I'm sorry, he's in the quiet room.'

RACISM

The idea of race originally came from the work of Carolus Linnaeus, an eighteenth-century Swedish botanist. He generated a system of classifying people that was based on outward appearance and this system was later used to create the classifications of Negroid, Caucasoid and Mongoloid. Racism is based on these classifications. They are used to divide humankind up into races, each with different origins and characteristics.

But science has moved on since then and DNA comparisons have completely overturned the idea of separate human races. What we know now is that all human beings are closely related. We share the same ancestors; people who left Africa a mere one to two hundred thousand years ago. Race has *no* foundation in biology – or any other branch of science. It is a myth, a fiction. Yet racism, far from being a fiction, is a harsh and persistent reality in our workplaces.

Racism, or rather, discrimination on the grounds of ethnicity, starts to rear its ugly head when you tell each other jokes about Irish or Polish people. It shows its face when the dress code of your workplace stops you from practising your religious beliefs. It's there in all its deformity when you miss out on

> *'I suffer from an incurable disease – colour blindness.'*
> Joost de Blank

promotion because of the way that you look or dress or speak. This discrimination can be direct – as when you are subject to racist abuse – or indirect – as when there is a general workplace instruction not to wear headgear and your religious beliefs require you to wear a turban, yarmulka or hijaab. All of these and other ways of discriminating come about because people choose to perpetuate the myth of race.

Here are some ideas about what you can do about this racism:

- Check out your own attitudes. Make sure that you're not guilty of putting some of the people around you in a box – one with a racist label on it – rather than seeing them as individuals.
- Check out the way others around you behave; think about the rules and regulations of your workplace. If you think these are racist or discriminatory, say so.

- If you are subject to racism or discrimination for any reason then keep a record of incidents. Log what was said or done, dates, times, details and witnesses.

- If it's direct racism, confront the person, tell them quietly, politely but assertively (*see* **Assertion**) that you take issue with their behaviour and should it happen again you'll make a formal complaint.

- If you can't manage doing that on your own, check (quietly and discreetly) with other people in your workplace. You may find that you've more support than you thought you had. You may even find that others are suffering too. If that's so, then see the person as a group and make sure he or she understands that you all take issue with his or her behaviour.

- Try to avoid being alone with someone who has made racist remarks to you in the past.

- Find out if your employer has a policy on or guidelines on racism or discrimination. If they haven't, ask for one to be created.

- If your confrontation hasn't worked then take the evidence that you've gathered to an independent third party. Make sure that it's someone with power or authority such as a labour union official, an equal opportunities, welfare, health and safety or personnel manager in your organization, or a respected member of your local community such as a pastor or priest. Make sure that the information that you give them is objective, factual and untainted by any suggestion of ambition or malice on your part.

- Remember, *nobody* has the right to discriminate against you because of the way that you look, the way you speak, or your cultural, or ethnic background or religious beliefs.

REASONS TO BE CHEERFUL

Most of you will have a whole string of reasons for feeling down, sad or bad about working in your own particular organization. If it's not the boss, it's that person in the next cubicle or office. If it's not them, it's the peanuts they pay you and if it's not the peanuts, then it's the fact that they expect you to create miracles with not enough staff and with clapped-out equipment.

But what about the good things? What about the reasons that keep you coming back here to struggle against insuperable odds to do a more than halfway decent job? These, believe it or not, are *your* reasons to be cheerful about working in your particular organization. They're worth writing down – if only so that you can revisit them when the going gets tough. So let's do that:

My reasons for being cheerful about working here are:

1

2

3

4

5

If you've got to here and can't think of any reasons to be cheerful about working in your organization, then take a break and come back later. If you come back later and still can't find any reasons, then see **To Boldly Go** or **Re-invention**.

We all know, or have heard about, people who seem to have the knack or the ability to shift lanes at least once – and sometimes several times – in their working lives. These are the people who start their working lives as bankers and then, suddenly and in the midst of apparent success, become opera singers. They start as chemical engineers, then switch lanes first to become management consultants, then lecture at a university business school and then, finally, set up a successful market garden. They fail in none of these roles – they succeed in them all. Our reactions to all of this lane shifting are mixed. For some of you it seems rather fickle. These lane-shifters, you tell yourselves – often with a touch of envy – are changeable, inconsistent, inconstant or unreliable. 'Why can't they settle down?' you ask. For others of you, it's admiration, sometimes wonder, that colours your comments. You see these lane-shifters as polymaths – people whose skills and knowledge span the divides between different subjects, people who are, as the dictionary says 'acquainted with various subjects'. In fact, the truth lies between these two extremes. For these lane-shifters aren't unique or brilliant people. What they've done is really quite ordinary and it's something that you can do if you want to. They've re-invented themselves.

The ability to re-invent yourself can be a key skill in your survival strategy. It'll enable you to stretch your skills, to use them to their utmost. You'll use it to jump out of those dead-end jobs or organizations that can trap and hold you. You'll use it to make sure that work becomes *fun*. But re-inventing yourself or switching lanes is about more than just changing jobs. For it's an expression of your individuality, a statement that says that you are *you* – rather than an engineer, lawyer, accountant or social worker.

To do it successfully you have to put quite a lot of preparation in; you have to judge carefully the when and to where of your lane jump and, most important, you have to be really clear about what you're going to take with you. But doing all of this isn't as difficult as it might seem. Start by taking these steps:

- ■ Stop reminding yourself what you can't do, and
- ■ Start asking what you *can* do.
- ■ Get some straight answers to these questions:
    - – What turns you on – and why?

   – What makes you feel great when you do it?

   – What epitaph would you like on your tombstone?

If you're honest, then the answers that you give to these questions will tell you what your core skills really are, what it is that makes you the unique individual that you are.

■ Check out your answers with someone who really knows you and who's prepared to be ruthlessly honest with you.

■ If their answers are different review your own answers and go through the loop again.

■ Continue until you've got a single sentence that describes you and your core skills. This must not say where you use them but what results they get.

Now you've got your core skill list. It's important that you get this list right – it's these skills, abilities and enthusiasms that will enable you to shift from one lane to another. It's also a list that forms the core of your cv or résumé (*see* **Résumés and Other Stories**). Now you need to look for the role or job that has a link with this list. Finding that will take time and won't be easy. But it will be worthwhile. It may be in your current organization or in a new one, it may be one that's in the area that you're currently working in or one that really does enable you to switch lanes. Once you've found it you'll be able to sell yourself with confidence and enthusiasm knowing that you're really selling your unique and special bundle of talents.

HOW NOT TO No. 8: PEOPLE MANAGEMENT
The Ways and Means of Bad People Management

■ Be rough and tough.

■ Remember feedback doesn't count, you know best – always.

■ Don't listen to them, just talk over them.

■ Always be critical and demanding.

■ Remember sensitivity is for wimps.

■ Lose your temper often – it keeps them on their toes.

■ Get moody so they don't know how you'll be.

■ Never, ever, admit your mistakes.

■ Always pass the blame and the buck – downwards.

■ Use people as stepping stones on your way to the top.

■ Arrogance and manipulation are *GOOD* – use them at least once a day.

■ Remember that the strong stand alone.

RELAXEZ-VOUS

Being able to relax – and do it well – is a real skill. Once you've got the knack you'll be able to relax anywhere. You can relax for one minute, two minutes or twenty minutes – it's up to you. Relaxing well is a skill that will be a major contributor to your survival rating. It'll reduce your stress level, help you to be effectively assertive and make you more adaptable and responsive in your dealings with customers and co-workers (*see* **Winding Up and Winding Down**; **Assertion**; **Adaptability**; **Customers**). But, as is so with all skills, it takes time and practice to be able to get to the point where you can relax well.

Being relaxed isn't about going all limp and floppy; it's actually a dynamic, adaptive state balanced between arousal and repose. There are all sorts of ways of getting into that state. Whichever one you use, it will always start with you preparing yourself. Get yourself physically comfortable with your legs and arms uncrossed. Then slow your breathing until it's easy and regular. Now you're ready to start. Try this one:

- First, tense your body – clench your fists and make a face.
- Hold that tension for a few moments – notice how it feels.
- Then exhale, let it go – completely – and relax.
- Now tense your body again – only half as much as the first time.
- Hold it, recognize it, feel the pull of your muscles.
- Then exhale, let it go, relax, feel the warmth of your body.
- Now tense your body again – only half as much as the last time.
- Hold it, feel the subtle pulls and twists in your back and neck.
- Then exhale; let it go, relax.
- Now tense only your mind.
- Then breathe, let yourself be free.

The more you do this, the better you'll get at it.

RÉSUMÉS AND OTHER STORIES

When is a résumé not a résumé? Answer: When it's an autobiography. Your résumé, curriculum vitae, cv or work record is something that you're often asked for. This happens when you apply for jobs in other companies, when you try to sell your services as a consultant or when you submit a book proposal to a publisher. In all of these and other circumstances, your résumé, cv or work record should give the person who reads it a quick rundown on your work record so far. As such, its content and style are important. If you get it right, you'll give that potential employer the message that you are worth the time and trouble of him or her interviewing you. If you get it wrong, then it's yet another lost opportunity that you face. But let's be realistic; a good cv – on it's own – won't get you a job, book contract or a consultancy assignment. What it will get you is the interview that could lead to all of those and more. So getting it right is important. Doing that is a surprisingly easy thing to do. Here are some key points to help you to do just that:

- Do your research thoroughly – make sure that you get your facts right, don't claim something you haven't got or didn't do.
- Identify your achievements – keep them short and sharp, cite measures of success where you can.
- Start with personal details – name, age, dob, qualifications, marital status, children (ages but not names), contact details.
- List jobs in reverse chronology – current job first, month/year of dates.
- Identify successes – 'major achievements' heading followed by at least three bullet points outlining your successes.
- Limit length – maximum of three sides A4.
- Other achievements – identify, briefly, at end.
- Edit, edit and edit – first impressions count, polish until totally error free, attractive and interesting.
- Update – review your résumé every 90 days and update as required.
- Repackage – revise and edit your cv for each job advert, refocus material so that relevant experience is highlighted and don't forget to add salary information if requested.
- Covering letter – short (3 paragraphs maximum), focused on how your experience meets their needs.

RISK

When you risk something – you take a chance. You expose yourself to uncertainty, to the possibility that things might not work out the way that you hope they will. The actions you take could lead to failure, loss and injury – or to success. If you feel that risk should be avoided, at all costs, then what you have to face is the fact that uncertainty and risk will, like birth and death, always be with us. There will always be alternatives that you hadn't thought of, events that you didn't foresee and information that wasn't available when you took your risk. None of your ventures will ever be risk-free. So, being able to develop and use the ability to face risk and use it to your advantage is important. In fact, it's so important that it's a key factor in your survival strategy.

For many of you, uncertainty and risk are negative, to-be-avoided, factors. They provoke anxiety, raise your stress levels, make you nervous. Your instincts tell you to delay, to step aside from situations where they abound. You yearn to strike out for the high ground of apparent certainty. But uncertainty and risk are relative.

> 'They who lose today may win tomorrow.'
> Cervantes

For what is risk to you can be – and often is – opportunity for others. Similarly, what is threatening and uncertain to others can be – and often is – challenging for you. When you find the way to face up to all this uncertainty and risk then not only do you increase your survival rating – you also open up an opportunity to gain advantage.

So how can you do this, how can you reduce or limit the risk of the torpedoes of chance sinking your ship? To do this you have to:

- Get into and accept the twin ideas of Cause and Consequence, and then
- Take the three steps of:
  1 Identifying the type, level and source of foreseeable risk
  2 Reducing or eliminating that risk
  3 Deciding whether or not you will accept the risk that remains.

If you look at this sequence in more detail what you'll find is that the first step – that of identifying the nature, level and source of your risk – can be a lengthy and difficult process. But it's one that's worthwhile. You can do it in one of two ways: either you look at the cause of the risk first, and then look at its consequences – as in what might happen and what would then follow, or you look, first, at consequences of a risk occurring and then look at the causes of that risk – as in what is an undesirable outcome and how might it be caused.

An example of the first of these – looking first at a cause and then at its consequences – occurs when you ask 'What happens if the boss turns down my project?' or 'What happens if I don't get that raise this year?' Then you identify and list the consequences that would follow. When you look at the second of these – the one that looks at consequences first and then identifies the possible causes – you'll start by asking 'What might cause me not to get that raise?' or 'What might lead the boss to turn down my project?' You'd then go on to list the possible causes. Some of these causes and consequences you can do something about. Eliminating these will take you a long way down the road to reduced risk.

But it's not enough just to identify the nature, level and source of your risks – you also need to assess whether – or not – they will happen. You can do this by either estimating the likelihood of the cause happening or by estimating the likelihood of the consequence occurring once the cause has happened. The easiest ways of doing this involve either comparing them to other similar risks or by drawing from your experience of identical or similar risks. Questions such as 'Have I done this before?', 'Has this happened before?' or 'Have I done this in this way before?' will help you to assess the level of risk involved. Once you've generated these estimates then you can use them to assess the combination of the probability of a risk occurring and the consequences of its occurrence. This gives you, even if you have to guess the probability, a basis on which you can decide whether or not to attempt to reduce the risk. For example, the low probability of the reactor of a town-centre nuclear power plant going critical and exploding may mean that it is likely to occur only once in one hundred years. But, if it did occur, several million people would die. As this consequence is unacceptable you'd need to reduce the chances of that risk actually occurring.

But in the end, however well you work towards reducing the level of risk, you'll still have to face the fact that an element of risk will never go away. The last and final step involves you deciding which risk you're prepared to take. Doing this takes skill and ability – as you'll see elsewhere in these pages (*see* **Decisions**).

SECONDMENTS

This involves you stepping out of your line position – the one you're used to and usually feel safe in – and taking on a new but temporary role with a different set of responsibilities. This role can be a full-time or a part-time one, it can be located in the same office block as your old job or involve a move to distant Anchorage and can involve hours, weeks, months or years of your working life.

The first thing to do if you're offered a secondment, special project or working party is to check its why and what. Find out what you can about its political background. Check out whether it's a real working party or special project – rather than a paper exercise commissioned so that justice is being seen to be done or to buy time for some other more realistic proposal. If its credentials stand up to scrutiny then you need to decide if this is the secondment for *you*. In doing this you've got to ask – and get some answers to – some pretty important questions; questions such as:

- What will I get out of it?
- What special experience will I gain?
- Will I get due credit if it goes right or all the blame if it goes wrong?
- Who will I be working for? What's their track record or background?
- Will I be able to get out if it all goes pear-shaped?
- What happens when it's all over – will my job be there or will it be the uncertainty of a new and, as yet, undefined role?
- What happens to my workload if it's a part-time role?

The answers that you get to these questions are really important. Get them wrong and you could find yourself stuck on a dead-end project that has little chance of succeeding. Get them right and you'll find you're on a secondment that, at its end, will leap-frog you over the heads of your contemporaries into a new, exciting and more responsible role.

If the answers look OK, then the next step is to find out about the downside of this secondment. For downside there will be. It may involve you in giving up your place in the local cricket team or golf tournament – because you'll have to fly to Aberdeen or Tulsa every Sunday afternoon. It may mean that you'll be staying in hotels for weeks, even months. It could mean that you lose touch with your friends or become sidelined in your family. You'll have to cope with feeling lonely, isolated, forgotten and out of touch with what's happening back home. So make sure that you, your partner and your family are realistic about all of this. Resist and keep on resisting any pressure to cut down on time at home or on home office keeping-in-touch visits and meetings. If when you've done all this, answered all of these questions, you still want to take on the working party, secondment or special project, then do so – positively and with enthusiasm.

But what if you don't want to go or don't like the way you've been told that you're going – rather than asked if you'd like to go? What should you do then? If this really is the case then you should:

- not take on something that you aren't completely positive about;
- get together the facts about why you aren't going;
- thank them for offering you this opportunity;
- tell them the difficulties it raises for you;
- then, say no – politely, but firmly.

This sequence, if you get it right, will either lead to a better offer – more support, travelling time, etc. or an acceptance that you really don't want to go – this time. There are, however, some organizations that will respond by giving you a this-will-damage-your-career reaction or even the go-or-be-sacked ultimatum. What this tells you is that it wouldn't have been a good move anyway and that it's time to move on – to another organization (*see* **To Boldly Go**).

SECRETS

You all have secrets – and some of you will have more than others! These secrets can be about anything that you do, say or think and about any part of your life. The number and nature of these secrets will shift and change with the seasons, tides and currents of your life. Some of them will be long-lived while others will have short ephemeral lives. Broadly speaking, there are two sorts of secret:

■ those that you keep *about* yourself, and
■ those that you keep *for* others.

Amongst the first of these you'll find the secrets of your private thoughts, hopes and desires – some of which might make you feel ashamed, guilty or embarrassed if they were exposed. But these aren't the only secrets that you keep about yourself: there are also those that you keep in order to gain advantage over others. Here you'll find secrets about your individual ambitions, what you intend to do to fulfil them, who in the organization you love or hate or who you bear a grudge against.

In the second group of secrets – those you keep for others – are those secrets that you keep for your organization. These will include things like the detail of plans for the launch of a new product, takeover plans or data about profit margins. But in this group are also the secrets that other people shared with you. This might happen when they are in stress or distress, when they are seeking advice or support or when they need to talk. Your possession of these secrets might cause you difficulty, joy or distress.

> *'Nothing is so burdensome as a secret.'*
> French proverb

Sharing a secret with someone else involves risk. For the more people who are 'in' on a secret – whatever sort it is – the greater is the risk of its exposure. When this happens, the trust that has maintained and protected that secret is broken. If the secret that is revealed is one that you kept about yourself or is a secret shared with you by someone else then its exposure can be seen as an act of betrayal (*see* **Betrayal**). But when the secrets of your organization are revealed the act of exposure is called a 'breach of confidence' and might result in dismissal or legal action.

But, despite all this, the secret is under attack. The front pages of our newspapers shout out the historic events of our politicians' 'private' lives, employees 'out' the pricing strategies of pharmaceutical companies and activists make public their opinions of the sexual inclinations of public figures. In the United States, organizations not only feel able to test their employees for the use of hard or soft drugs – such as cocaine or marijuana – but also for the use of tobacco and alcohol. You are observed and recorded in your workplace by what are called 'security' cameras and the equipment that you use in your job is routinely and remotely monitored. Your telephone calls are recorded and your e-mails (*see* **E-mail**) and internet access are monitored. But this campaign against the secret has its advantages for you. For now you can gain access to what others record or write about you. Now, for example, you can see your medical records, credit 'ratings' and the files and records that employers keep about you.

But, despite all these changes, it looks as if at least some of your secrets are going to remain yours for the foreseeable future. Perhaps, then, what you need is a bit of risk limitation. Ask yourself which of your secrets you really *need* to continue to hold on to – and why. Increase your survival rating by getting rid of those of your secrets that are worn out or no longer relevant – and travel light.

SELF STUFF

The self-factors – self-control, self-awareness and self-assurance – can all be important contributors to your survival plan. So let's take a look at them, one at a time:

Self-control

This is about staying cool when everybody else is getting hot. When you've got it – and know how to use it – you're able to stay composed, calm and confident, even in the heat of a crisis.

Excessive self-control leads to rigidity, an inability to adapt and a hatred of change. People who have absolute and total control of their feelings are either emotionally damaged or robots – neither of which seem much fun.

Self-awareness

If you really are self-aware then you are:

- tuned into your strengths and weaknesses,
- able to translate your experiences into learning, and
- open to feedback from others.

Getting more self-aware is worthwhile. But self-awareness in excess is not good. It can lead to an unhealthy obsession with feedback – the 'how-was-that-for-you' syndrome – and tendency to become confused about what's the real world. It is, of course, the real world – or rather your organization's version of it – that you're trying to survive – isn't it?

Self-assurance

Self-assurance is that quality that you don't have very often but everybody else seems to have all the time. When you are self-assured you're able to communicate well and conduct yourself with confidence. Too much self-assurance, however, is only good if you want to be a used car dealer or promote junk bonds.

The phrase 'silent majority' is used to describe either those who are dead, or those people whose views remain unexpressed. Most organizations have silent majorities. They are usually, but not always, described as being silent because they don't express their views about what's happening or should happen in the organization. They remain silent because:

■ they are complacent or disinterested, or

■ they aren't encouraged or even allowed to express their views about the organization.

Both of these are redolent of bad management, management that isn't bothered about or doesn't care about what people think or feel about what's going on in an organization. This can come about for a number of reasons. It may be because of the organization's culture and history (*see* **Archaeology – Corporate**), or it may be because there's no means or mechanism by which these views can be expressed. But, in the twenty-first century, situations like this are few and far between. So when organizations with silent majorities do exist it's often because of the dominant position and views of some or all of the managers (*see* **Dominance**). In these organizations the silent majority is encouraged to remain silent. To be other than this, to ask questions or say 'Why?' is frowned upon, even suppressed, by managers whose rule is seen as being above challenge.

Managing people in this way isn't just bad – it's also lazy. For the people who work for an organization *are* that organization. It's a very rare event for them to be without opinions or views about the way that organization is being run. If you're a manager, you ignore these views and opinions at your peril. If you're being managed – and find yourself in a silent majority situation – then you've really only got two choices. You can:

■ go – to an organization that listens to and cherishes its people (*see* **To Boldly Go**), or

■ stay – and try to open an informal communication channel with your manager (*see* **Communication**; **Influence – or Power?**; **Grapevines**).

SINGING

Singing doesn't happen much in our organizations. But singing can be – and often is – a good thing to do. It opens your lungs, expands your chest muscles, improves your breathing and enables you to express your emotions in ways not possible by the use of ordinary speech. Singing is also very versatile. You can do it on your own or do it with any number of other people. Your singing can be happy or sad, quiet or loud. You can sing spontaneously or after rehearsal and preparation. In short, singing – like laughter and dancing – is good for us (*see* **Laughter**). So why don't you sing in your organization?

The answer to this comes in two parts. The first of these is that singing isn't part of the conventions of our day-to-day communication. You don't – unless, that is, you're in an Italian opera – sing questions at each other or sing instructions to one another. You may shout, speak, even whisper these – but you don't sing them. But the reasons why you use speech rather than singing for these sorts of communication aren't that obvious. After all, birds sing at each other – and often do so in situations that are much more life-and-death than those that occur in your organization. When you think about this you'll soon get to the second part of the answer as to why you don't sing in your organization. That is, quite simply, that when you sing you almost always do so to express your emotions. When you do that you expose your inner feelings. You might even, occasionally, be seen as being 'out of control'. Most organizations aren't comfortable with either being 'out of control' or emotions. Conflict and its cousin, anger, are suppressed and compassion and caring are too soft, too 'girlie', too 'touchy-feely' to survive the 'real' world (*see* **Caring**; **Compassion**). Control is king in these organizations (*see* **Freaks – Control and Other**) and real genuine emotions are suppressed, sublimated or, at best, expressed very indirectly. But what they – or rather their people – miss is the joy of a swift chorus from Queen's *Bohemian Rhapsody* or Handel's *Messiah* when things are going really well. You don't have to be able to sing well – you just have to be able to sing. Try it.

STAKEHOLDERS

Organizations are about people. It's their creativity, adaptability and energy that takes an organization from birth to success and it's their skills and abilities that plot, plan and manage an organization's passage towards its goals and targets (*see* **Organizations**). However, the people who influence these goals and targets aren't just those who work for that organization. The term 'stakeholder' is often used to describe this larger group of people who can exert, in some way, influence on your organization.

To be a stakeholder you have to have something to gain or lose by the way the organization performs. This throws the net in a pretty wide arc. For example, the stakeholders for a community hospital would include medical and non-medical employees, community doctors, volunteers, suppliers, patients, local elected representatives, the community, social services staff, regional health authority, government agencies, contractors and subcontractors and taxpayers. This tells us that a typical list of stakeholders will involve many different roles and groups from beyond the formal boundaries of the organization. It will include anyone whose interests or 'stake' are affected by the actions of the organization.

Stakeholders can gain or lose by the actions of the organization. These gains and losses can be direct – as in the case of an employee – or indirect – as in the case of a local shopkeeper or businessman. Similarly, they all have needs and desires which will, directly and indirectly, reach out to influence the goals, aims and objectives of the organization. But these needs and desires will often be in conflict with one another and with the needs and desires of the organization. Stakeholders are important – in some cases, just as important as the organization's stockholders. Becoming aware of that is a significant step on your road to survival in your organization. For it will give you a view of your organization that extends beyond its formal boundaries. And that is where your future lies (*see* **Your Future**).

Getting and staying healthy can make a very big contribution to your survival. Exercise helps you to resist and throw off the negative effects of excessive stress (*see* **Winding Up and Winding Down**) and the right diet keeps you in trim so that you can cope with the ups and downs of life in the organizations of the twenty-first century. Finding the right exercise pattern and the right diet for you are both investments in your future – so spend time talking to experts and reading up on your options. In the meantime, here are some ideas to start you off on the road to being healthy and fit:

■ Start off your fitness campaign modestly – by using the stairs instead of the lift, by walking instead taking a cab.

■ Gentle rhythmic exercise is good – walking, swimming, cycling or jogging.

■ When you're waiting – for someone to answer the phone or for the train to arrive – breathe in and out deeply and slowly.

■ Eat well – with lots of fruit and vegetables.

■ Reduce your caffeine intake. Try drinking water or fruit juice instead.

■ Avoid alcohol at lunch time – it'll lead to an afternoon attention trough – and drink moderately out of work.

■ Get your weight down to a figure that's right for you.

■ Drop the chocolate bar or cookie snacks – try nuts or dried fruit instead.

■ Check your desk posture and get yourself a good chair.

■ Get a life outside the office – play sport, swim, dance, join a choir – do something that you enjoy.

■ Take weekend breaks – book them well ahead – to give yourself something to look forward to.

■ Get a regular physical check-up – and use it to talk to your doctor about you and your job.

■ Find relaxation techniques that work for you – and use them (*see* **Relaxez-Vous**).

The twenty-first century, dot.com world that you live and work in seems to have a face that's turned, most of the time, towards the future. It's constantly looking forward, striving to catch a glimpse of – and grasp – a tomorrow that will be full of new products, new technology and new opportunities. But in all this enthusiasm to move on, to become, as it were, tomorrow today, what's forgotten is that there is a thread that links your past, present and future. This is the thread of continuity between what you hope might happen in the future and what has happened in the past. Your guides as to this thread are the storytellers of your organization.

There always have been storytellers. They sat by the campfires of the distant past, telling of kings, heroes and nations. With the printing press, their stories became written, accessible to many – instead of verbal, handed down from father to son. Their stories changed too. They shifted from being about what *had been* to what *ought to be*. Now their stories try to persuade us about what *might have been* and what *will be*. Our organizations are now defined by the memories that they do – and don't – want to keep alive. The storytellers have also changed. Once they held the key to the lessons of the past, now they draw their public relations cloaks around them and try to tell you what you ought to see in the present and the future. But all of this change isn't necessarily bad. For without the burden of the past you are free to cast your net where you will. Whether or not you fill that net often seems almost irrelevant. It is, as they say, the freedom to learn from your own mistakes that counts. But that isn't the only gift that untangling your feet from this thread of continuity with the past will give you. For once you take that step you are free to write your own individual story – your stories of the 'self' that is you. By doing this, you can free yourself from the prison that the organization has built around you and from the messages that others have given you about who you are. Try re-inventing yourself (*see* **Re-invention**) and become a hero in your own time.

SUCCESS

'The ability to chant a mantra to a bottom line beat.'

John Battelle

'Success – it's what you do with what you've got.'

Woody Hayes

'The key to success is never to do anything that's not interesting to you.'

James Lovelock

'The true key to success is knowing what features set you apart from the competition.'

Anita Roddick

'Eighty percent of success is showing up.'

Woody Allen

'Success always occurs in private, and failure in full view.'

Anon

'Success is that old ABC – Ability, Breaks and Courage.'

Charles Luckman

'Success seems to be largely a matter of hanging on after others have let go.'

William Feather

'The Two Rules of Success 1. Don't tell everything you know.'

Anon

'The key to success is simple – make people dream.'

Gerald de Nerval

'Success is the result of perfection, hard work, learning from failure, loyalty to those for whom you work and persistence.'

Colin Powell

| # TALL POPPIES

The phrase 'tall poppies' was first used in Australia. Originally it described the privileged or distinguished members of the society – and came about because of the habit of carving poppy heads on the top of church pew seat ends – a pew that would be owned by a wealthy family. But times have changed and in the twenty-first century the phrase is more often used to describe those people who stand out from the crowd – not just because of wealth, but also because of their skills, ideas, creativity or opinions.

In your organization, the tall poppies are those people with an above average strike rate – but a different way of doing things. They are the eccentrics (*see* **Eccentricity**) who use their skill and creativity to do their 'own thing' – often to the organization's benefit but also in defiance of its rules (*see* **Unwritten Rules**). These tall poppies are rarely loved and cared for. They excite envy, the determination to pull them down, cut off their heads – irrespective of the quality (*see* **Quality**) or value of what they generate. In many organizations tall poppies are barely tolerated. When they are the tolerance often only extends as far as the tall poppy's first mistake – at which point he or she is brought to task for their 'deviant' behaviour. None of this makes any sense at all – unless, that is, you're a control freak.

For tall poppies can often see further than you can and sometimes – if you let them – they can tell you about better, more effective (*see* **Efficiency and Effectiveness**), more adaptable (*see* **Adaptability**) ways of doing things. But if you're a tall poppy – take care! For the control freaks of your organization will be after you (*see* **Freaks – Control and Other**). You'll know these freaks by their acts. For what these control freaks want is a culture of blame – a 'no' culture hidden under the cloak of accountability – rather than a 'yes' culture in which creativity and enthusiasm are encouraged, accepted or nurtured (*see* **Bosses – Not So Good; Bosses – Terrible**). To survive their predations, you are going to have to develop good camouflage and be pretty fast on your feet (*see* **Empowerment; Grapevines; Lateral Thinking; Re-invention**).

The word 'team' is used a lot in organizations. You'll have sales teams, assembly teams, clean-up teams, problem-solving teams, project teams, management teams – and more! Team working has become one of those must-do features of the organizations of the twenty-first century. This has happened because, at its best, the team enables your organization to tap into and use people's skills, abilities and creativity. When you get that happening, and happening well, what you get is a team that can:

- make things happen – quicker and better;
- create solutions to problems;
- find ways of moving a whole organization up a gear.

If all of this happens – you've got a good team. A team like this is a good place to work in. You'll find that it's flexible and adaptable and able to:

- grow and change to meet new demands;
- re-invent itself when individuals move on;
- be independent of the skills and abilities and even the absence of any one member.

This team can be about almost anything. It can be:

- a working team – that makes or does things;
- a special purpose or project team – that's formed to solve particular problems or to carry out specific tasks;
- a multifunctional team – that has members from all over the organization and is focused on problems or projects of common interest;
- a self-directed team – that doesn't have a permanent leader and in which the task of leadership is shared.

All of these teams – whatever their purpose or nature – have something in common. They all consist of people who collaborate, who work together in ways that are aimed at achieving a common goal. They have team members with shared purposes who work

> 'A team is more difficult to study than a person.'
> R. Meredith Belbin

together co-operatively to generate outcomes that are collective – rather than individual. All of this is very different from the work-groups of your organization. In these you each carry out your individual task under someone's supervision. You have a purpose that's common – rather than shared – and you undertake individual actions in order to bring about or create outcomes that reflect your individual choices and desires.

But teams aren't always good – they can also fail. These teams are dominated by a powerful few, they lack the basic skills and abilities needed for the tasks they face and they get so locked into their task that they become insulated from the truths of the real world outside. These – the teams of our failures – are not good places to work in.

Here are some tips on how to make sure that failure doesn't come for your team:

- If you're the team leader of a new team:
    - make sure that you're heavily involved in choosing the team members;
    - when you do that make sure that you get people with prior experience of successful teams;
    - make sure that you get a blend of functional skills that's right for the team task;
    - build a team of people with interpersonal skills, problem-solving skills and decision-making skills.
- If you're taking over an old team, work hard to make sure that you get to know and understand your team members.
- Remember that, new or old, it's not *your* team, it's *our* team.
- If you're a team member:
    - work hard to make sure that you contribute to building that 'team spirit' that makes a team great;
    - share your knowledge and experience, work hard to make sure that these are accessible to others;
    - take on tasks that develop and extend your communication, problem-solving and decision-taking skills;
    - when the going gets tough hang on in there – a good team is worth fighting for.

TESTING TIMES

It used to be that when you applied for a job you went through a sequence that went something like application form → interview → offer. This has changed. Now you have to jump through an additional hoop – that of psychometric testing. These 'mind-measuring' or psychometric tests are widely used in organizations. It would be unusual for you *not* to have to take one or two of them before or after any job interview. Your potential employer will use them for a number of reasons – but mainly because they will tell him or her whether you can do a particular job or whether you will – or won't – fit into the organization. There isn't just one sort of test – you can get a test to measure almost anything. Here are some examples:

- attainment tests – aimed at measuring knowledge and skills;
- intelligence tests – focused on intellectual potential and problem-solving skills;
- aptitude tests – can you spell, do sums, recognize shapes and sizes, order and classify things and do you have manual dexterity?;
- personality tests – claim to measure temperament and disposition;
- interest tests – claims to relate interest areas to suitability for certain kinds of work.

Most of these are pencil-and-paper tests run against the clock under supervised conditions. Some, however, involve observations of you working with other people in a set situation. Acceptance of the methods and results of these tests is by no means universal and a continuing debate – particularly about personality tests – surrounds the value of their use. They do, however, represent an alternative to the interview, one that is standardized, systematic, thorough and consistent – all of which the interview often isn't. But their ability to predict how you will perform in a particular job in an organization is, at best, limited.

So, given that it's difficult to avoid these tests, how can you use them to your best advantage? The first thing to recognize is that you can't 'beat' a test. Indeed, if you try to do that what you will find is that your results will be seen as inconsistent. This is because most of the tests have series of 'checkback' questions – to assess the consistency of your answers – built into them. It's better that you accept that you're going to have to take these tests and, having done that, aim to 'give it your best'. Here are some tips to help you to do just that:

- Before the test day:
  - read all the explanatory material you've been sent;
  - do the practice questions given until you get them right;
  - relax.
- On the test day:
  - eat normally;
  - visit the washroom before the test;
  - make sure that you've everything that you need (the test centre will provide pens or pencils);
  - arrive early – but not too early;
  - when you're sitting down in the test room make sure that you're comfortable – loosen your tie, belt etc. and take your shoes off;
  - relax.
- The test:
  - listen to and read the instructions carefully; if you don't understand ask;
  - make sure that you know how to fill the form in and how long you've got to do that;
  - the more questions you answer, the higher your mark;
  - don't get hung up on questions that you can't answer – make an intelligent guess or move on;
  - keep an eye on the clock;
  - ignore how fast or slow the people around you seem to be working;
  - if you're doing a personality test read the questions carefully, be as honest as you can, and trust your first impressions;
  - keep going, but sit up and look around occasionally;
  - if you finish early, go back and check over your answers;
  - remember that you can only do your best.

Your test results shouldn't be taken to be an absolute measurement of you or your abilities. Beware if your interviewer seems to put too much value on your test results – you may find that that particular organization is either full of people who are good at personality tests or all seem to have fallen out of the same mould.

THIRTY-FIVE PLUS

There comes a time, for most of us, when we begin to feel that maybe, just maybe, we aren't going to scale the dizzy heights of those brave, bright ambitions that we had when we were young. This is rarely a sudden, instant revelation. It surfaces gradually, quietly, in the early hours. You slowly realize that all the late nights and weekends of working on those reports haven't paid off; you see a younger man or woman – who joined the firm after you and has less experience than you have – getting the promotion that you had your eye on. For most of you this wake-up call kicks in somewhere between the age of thirty-five and forty. By then, you'd told yourself all those years ago, you should – if you were going to make it – have scaled the dizzy heights of departmental chief or some such. By then, you should have 'made your mark'. Realizing that you aren't going to 'make your mark' is one of those 'rites of passage' that we all experience and that sociologists and psychologist are so fond of writing about. It's like your first girlfriend or boyfriend, your first sports car or your first promotion. Except that all those were probably good – while this isn't.

Facing the reality that you aren't going to 'make it' – at least on this track – isn't easy. The future you face seems stark, limited and unfulfilling. You feel that if you switch lanes and start again, you'll be in competition with bright, enthusiastic, younger people. But is all that true, is the future really as bleak as that?

Of course, it isn't either that black or that bleak – but neither is it easy. For what you now face is a choice. Either you can use this realization to give you the energy that you need to reassess and reprioritize your life, or you can allow the weight of it to drive your head, ostrich-wise, further into the sand. You can choose to accept the reality that's emerged or you can ignore it. But before you decide what you're going to do, let's make one thing clear: that is that the corporate career, the guaranteed job-for-life, no longer exists. You are no longer able to rely on staying on the payroll just because you do a 'good job'. This means that the choice you face is actually an inevitable one and that you've been lucky that other events haven't triggered it earlier (*see* **Downsizing; We're Going To Have To Let You Go**).

So what are you going to do? If your choice is to ignore what's happening and to bury your head further in the sand, then I suggest you read no further. But before you close this book, and push your head down into the dark again, remember to leave the book close at hand – ready for when events beyond your control drag you – kicking and shouting – back into the real world. If your choice is to accept the emerging reality – congratulations! For getting real, seeing things as they really are is the first step on a pathway that will take you to somewhere else – a somewhere that will be different from where you are now but a somewhere that just might, if you work hard and get it right, be better.

To prepare for that here are some of the things you need to do:

- ■ Realize that your current job is transitory – one that will take you from where you are to where you want to be.
- ■ Identify what *you* want to do in the next year – be specific, set targets.
- ■ Review your skills, ability and experience against those targets.
- ■ Identify the gaps and work hard to fill them.
- ■ Review your résumé or cv (*see* **Résumés and Other Stories**).
- ■ Prepare to re-invent yourself (*see* **Re-invention**).
- ■ Get Ready – Steady – Go!

'My career development programme was going fine until I realized I forgot to buy volumes 2–10.'

TIMES A'WASTING

Time is a scarce resource – none of us ever seem to have enough of it. When this happens to you – and for some of you it happens *every* day – then you need to do something about it. Doing that – getting on top of your time and managing it well – is key to your struggle to survive your organization.

Here's how you can do it:

- Check out what you're actually doing, compare it to your job description and then get rid of the stuff that isn't your responsibility. But don't just dump it, talk to your boss about it – she or he may not realize you've been doing the photocopying in your lunch break – and then get someone junior to do the low grade stuff.

- Identify and prioritize the key areas of your work.

- Plan the how and when of these key tasks. Create a schedule – and stick to it. Set aside time when you won't be interrupted. Tell other people that you're not available at those times and get them to field your calls.

> 'Times is a file that wears and makes no noise.'
> English Proverb

- Don't tolerate interruptions, learn to say no.

- Make sure that you deal with the unscheduled tasks. Putting them aside won't make them go away, nor will it make them any smaller – so do them now.

- When crises occur make sure that you don't get swept up in a frenzy of unfocused activity. Step back, take a cool look at what's happened, prioritize what needs to be done, decide who's going to do it and by when (*see* **Delegation**).

- Monitor what's happening and be prepared to change your plans.

- Take breaks away from your desk.

Resigning from your job is something that you are going to do several times during your working lifetime. Your reasons for doing this will vary enormously. Most of the time it'll be because you've found another job that you feel offers you something that's lacking in your current job. That 'extra something' could be more money, different challenges, a chance to expand your experience, more or different responsibilities, a new start or even the chance to get out from under a bad or terrible boss (*see* **Bosses – Not So Good**; **Bosses – Terrible**). But, whatever the reason is, it's important that your resigning is done well. Getting it wrong can lead to bad gossip (*see* **Gossip**), recriminations (*see* **Vindictiveness**) and a bad reference. Getting it right involves:

Your letter of resignation

Putting a lot of thought and care into your letter of resignation is important. Apart from the basics – addressed to your boss, your name, date, notice of departure, date of departure and signature – this letter is also an opportunity to express, providing it's true, your appreciation of the support, help and opportunities that your boss has given you while you've worked under him or her. If it's not true then don't say it – but don't be rude or critical – keep to the basics. Whatever you say, make sure that the letter is typed up neatly and that you've kept a copy.

Keep it to yourself

Don't discuss this letter or its content with any of your co-workers until you've given it to your boss. Whatever you think of him or her it's discourteous that he or she should find out that you're leaving through the grapevine. Arrange to see him or her in their office.

Resignation interview

This interview will be different from most of the interviews that you experience. For one thing, your boss probably won't know what's coming. Expect a reaction. He or she may become upset or aggressive (*see* **Aggression**), or even tell you that you've betrayed them (*see* **Betrayal**). They could also express delight at your departure or act deadpan. Throughout all of this it's important that you keep your cool. Speak carefully and clearly, be co-operative. Stress your willingness to make sure that any handover goes well and that any uncompleted work or projects will be brought to an agreed conclusion.

Will you stay?

What happens when you hand your notice in is that your employers come face-to-face with the reality that you won't be around much longer. This can lead them to make a counter-offer or asking you how much would you want in order to stay? If this happens, and you're tempted to stay, don't be afraid to negotiate for more than they've put on the table and make sure that they put their offer in writing. But always, whether you are tempted or not, be courteous.

Co-workers

Whether or not your boss tells your co-workers that you're going is up to him or her. But once the interview is over make time to talk to all the people that you've worked with. If they've given you help and support – thank them for it and make sure you stay in touch with them. If they haven't been supportive or helpful, thank them anyway – but don't stay in touch.

Last day

Don't get drunk – remember last impressions are often the ones that last longest. If you think it's appropriate, buy or make a 'good-bye' cake to be shared out on the afternoon of your last day – but make sure it's a good one!

'Keep it to yourself . . . I'm leaving . . . but don't let the boss know.'

TOLERANCE

If you ask a group of co-workers how they get on they'll probably tell you 'Sure, we get on ok' or ' We've learned to live with each other' or even 'She puts up with me as long as I put up with her.' Most – but not all – of this is about tolerance. Tolerance – or your willingness to be patient, even indulgent, with each other's faults, opinions and habits – is a rare but important aspect of the way you behave. It's one that's much in demand in the diverse societies of the twenty-first century. For if humankind is to survive as a race then tolerance – of each other's belief systems, cultural values and religions – is needed. In your organizations, tolerance is just as significant. It lies at the core of any effective team (*see* **Teams**) and it's key to your survival. It allows, even encourages, the statement of opposing viewpoints, it enables a true consensus (*see* **Consensus**) to evolve without violence or destructive conflict. It enables you to work together.

Tolerance is about recognition – from a distance – and the belief that there's room enough for us all, rather than unconditional acceptance. What this means, in its simplest form, is that you aren't obliged to slurp your soup when you tolerate Fred slurping his. One of the easiest ways of identifying tolerance is, paradoxically, by its absence. For intolerance is about judgement and rejection. It denies your right to be different from each other. In its worst form, it is a narrow-minded or bigoted opposition to dissent. Intolerance rears its ugly head in your organization as racism, ageism, gender bias, harassment, bullying and domination – none of which are good, either for the organization or your survival rating (*see* **Racism**; **Glass Ceilings**; **Ageism**; **Bullying**; **Harassment**; **Dominance**). When these appear then they give notice that tolerance has, so to speak, 'left by the back door'.

But tolerance isn't just about benign acceptance. For your doctor will tell you that your body can acquire a form of tolerance to poisons or other drugs by being repeatedly exposed to low-level doses of them. As a result, your body's natural defensive response to that drug or poison becomes less, your body has learned to tolerate them. This is exactly what happens when you are continually exposed to low-level gender abuse, harassment or bullying. You develop a tolerance to that which should be *intolerable*. Be aware of this and check, at regular intervals, whether you're building up a tolerance to something that you shouldn't have to tolerate at all.

HOW NOT TO No. 9: NEW BROOM STRIKES OUT

Sandy wasn't sure whether or not to stay on when her old boss retired. She'd been his PA for six or more years and they'd got used to each other's ways of working. But when Dave – who had a reputation for being difficult – arrived she thought she'd give it a go. After all, he seemed pleasant enough. But, as the weeks went by, she became more and more uneasy. He was very demanding and she'd seen him being unreasonable and rude to other people. But, because he was generally OK with her, she stayed on. It all came to a head, however, when he came back from his holiday. While he was away she'd taken the opportunity to tidy up the filing system in his desk – something she's routinely done for her previous boss. Early in his first morning back she'd heard banging and shouting from his office and, against her better judgement, had gone in. What she found amazed her. He'd pulled out his desk's filing drawer and flung it across the office. Papers were strewn all over the place and he was angry – very angry. When he saw her standing there he shouted at her to get out and then – to her astonishment – picked up a soft drink can and threw it at her.

The bruise on her arm lasted for over a week – long enough for Sandy to get herself checked over by her doctor and to get a lawyer who was prepared to take on her case. The company settled out of court – but not before they'd tried to say that Sandy wasn't up to the job. Sandy moved on – another town, another job. Some years later she had the satisfaction of reading in the newspaper that Dave – who was now vice president in another larger company – had been sacked for 'conduct unbecoming to a senior manager'.

Learning and training go hand in hand – or, at least, they *ought* to. But, when you go on a training programme, does that always happen and, if so, does what you've learnt help you to do your job better? These, of course, are *the* big questions about training in organizations. Unfortunately the answer isn't always one that's unconditionally positive. You've all been on badly run, boring, training programmes that were irrelevant to what you did back in the workplace. Some of you might have been on programmes that fired you up, really got you going, only to find that no one was interested when you got back to work. But some of you have also been on programmes or courses that did make a difference, that were useful to you and your co-workers. So how can you make sure this happens every time you go on a training programme? To find the answer to this question you'll have to go back to basics – first, about learning and then second, about training.

Learning is *good*. It helps you to understand and engage with the world about you. When you're young you learn how to walk, talk, run, swim, read, spell and write. As you grow you learn how to use all of these and other skills in ways that help you to 'fit into' the social groups around you – to both your and their benefit. When you're old, learning new skills and abilities is one of the ways that you keep fit. It opens up new avenues for you, allowing you to revisit old interests and keeps your mind active. As a result of all this learning you change, often permanently, both what you do and the way that you do it. These changes become permanent and effective when you've practised what they involve and gained useful experience by doing so.

Training – or, at least, *good* training – is about giving you the opportunity to practise and, by so doing, to gain experience (*see* **Delegation**). But if it's going to work and be effective, then training has to have a focus, a purpose. And that's where you come in. For effective training isn't the sort of generalized cure-all that it's sometimes thought to be. Effective training is a focused, targeted activity, aimed at answering *your* needs.

So what are these needs and how do you find the course or programme that will answer them? Finding the answers to these questions is easier than you might think. Much of it you can do on your own or with the help of a friend. Here are the steps that you'll need to follow:

Step one: Identify your current skills

This is the foundation stone of your training programme and you must be both realistic and accurate when you do it. There's little point or value in claiming that you can do things that you can't or kidding yourself that you can do things better than you can. But, on the other hand, don't underrate yourself and remember to include both practical skills and those that you've learnt and used outside the workplace.

Step two: Identify the skills that your current job demands

To do this well you really need a job description of some sort. This tells you what are the tasks involved in doing the job and the skills needed to carry out those tasks. Again, be as realistic and specific as you can. Think about the skills that you can see will be needed in order to do this job in the near future but don't, at this stage, think about what you'll need for your next job. That comes later. If you haven't got a job description then sit down and compile a list of all the things that you do and then identify the skills that you use in doing them.

Step three: The skill gap

Your skill gap is the one that you see when you compare what you found in Step One to what you identified in Step Two. It's also individual and particular to you. It's your skill gap – not Fred's or Charlie's or Jill's – and if you're going to bridge it then it is *vital* that you accept and own it. When you've done that, set down your goals and priorities. Ask yourself questions such as 'Which comes first – learning about computers or learning bookkeeping?', or 'When do I learn this by?' – and get some answers. Write your answers down, generate a training plan for yourself and, when you're satisfied with it, move on to the next step.

Step four: Talk to the boss

The boss is the person who holds the training purse strings. If you're going to get your training needs answered you'll need to persuade him or her that your training needs are not only reasonable and realistic but that answering them will help you do your job better. If you've carried out Steps One to Three comprehensively and well, then you've both got the beginnings of what could be a very constructive dialogue. But remember his or her training budget isn't bottomless and you may have to accept some delays to your plan. But if the worst happens, if you don't get a constructive response, then don't give up. Revise your training programme, find some night school classes, find ways of answering your training needs from within your own resources.

Step five: Doing it

Choosing the 'right' training course is rather like choosing a good builder – personal recommendation works best. Ask around, find people who've been on courses like the one that you're interested in. Listen to what they say, think about it and then make your choice.

TRAINING CHECKLIST

The best sort of training is inspiring, even wonderful. The worst sort is boring, badly structured and a waste of time. Use this checklist to focus on how you feel about the last training session that you attended.

■ I knew what I wanted to learn: Yes ☐   No ☐

■ I understood what the training session
was supposed to teach me: Yes ☐   No ☐

■ Did what I wanted and the session's
objectives agree?   Yes ☐   No ☐

■ Was the session: well run?   Yes ☐   No ☐

■   interesting?   Yes ☐   No ☐

■   useful?   Yes ☐   No ☐

■ Did the session give me stuff that I
could use in the workplace?   Yes ☐   No ☐

■ Did it change the way I work?   Yes ☐   No ☐

■ Would I recommend this training
session to other people?   Yes ☐   No ☐

Total scores: Yes ☐ ____   No ☐ ____

If you got two or more Nos – then you wasted your time. Try not to repeat the experience!

When you trust somebody to do something what you're saying is that you accept – without any further evidence or guarantee – that they'll do what they say they're going to do. Doing this – trusting somebody – is, in its purest form, like matrimony or death – a leap in the dark. It's also a rare commodity. Most of the time, your trust is a conditional, half-hearted, unsure-of-itself affair. You're never quite sure whether they'll do it, you're uncertain as to how much you can say (*see* **Secrets**). You feel dubious of his or her motives, you're unwilling to take him or her at face value (*see* **Betrayal**). Most of this comes about because of your past experiences. You remember being disappointed, let down and deceived and you're unwilling to expose yourself to the risk of repeating that experience.

But trust is important. It lies at the core of all relationships, it's crucial to the way that teams work (*see* **Teams**) and it's one of those must-have factors that enable organizations to function. It's also crucial to your survival in those organizations. Increasing your trust and reducing its conditionality is important. But in the day-to-day hustle of your work-a-day world the leap into the dark of unconditional trust is an act that's neither sensible nor realistic. You have to negotiate your trust, mould its shape, form and limits on the anvil of experience. Doing that isn't easy, it takes time and effort. But here are some guide points to help you on your way:

- Keep your promises – if you can't, apologize, explain why (*see* **Promises**).
- Listen – more than you talk (*see* **Listening**).
- Co-operate – and share the credit for good results and the blame for bad ones
- Be fair – even if others are not fair with you.
- Try putting yourself in the other person's shoes (*see* **Empathy**).
- Own up when you get it wrong – and apologize (*see* **Mistakes**).
- Praise others when they get it right.
- Don't get locked into self-interest – look out for others.
- Check out changes with those who might be affected – before, not after, they happen (*see* **Change**).
- If you care for your co-workers, then show it (*see* **Caring**).

Rules are about regulation and control. They are about what you do and the way that you do it. All organizations have rules, whatever their size, culture or history. Most of these are written rules. But these are not the only rules which exist in your organization, nor are they the most potent of the rules that you are expected to conform to during your working hours. For there's another set of rules that are just as powerful as those that are written in these procedure manuals. These are the unwritten rules of your organizations.

The range and scope of these are enormous. They can, for example, be about your appearance at work – such as the clothes or jewellery that you wear, the style in which you have your hair cut and whether you do or don't have a beard or moustache. They might also be about your accent, the way that you talk or the sort of words you use. They can even include your table manners, the ways that you eat your food or the ways that you drink your tea or coffee. But, most of the time, they are about the ways in which you communicate with those around you in your organization. All organizations have unwritten rules about what is acceptable in terms of the style of these communications. For example, the unwritten rule might be that managers behave dominantly towards their subordinates but submissively towards their superiors (*see* **Pecking Order**). You'll not find this written down anywhere – but, nevertheless, it's what's expected. Similarly, people who talk freely about their feelings are frowned upon in many organizations. The unwritten rule about what's 'appropriate' says that people should be closed-lipped, secretive and undemonstrative. Your own experience will have told you that people who behave flamboyantly stand out and can be at more risk than people who 'fade into the wallpaper'. One of the key factors which seems to govern the acceptability – or unacceptability – of someone's personal style is to do with the way in which conflict is handled. Few organizations handle conflict well (*see* **Nose to Nose**). In most of them it is suppressed and buried, even ignored. The individual who strives to bring conflict out into the open and find ways of using it to the general good is often seen as a 'trouble maker' who is riding roughshod over an unwritten rule.

By now you will have realized that very few of the things that these unwritten rules are about are covered by your employment contract. But these unwritten rules are often more potent in their effect than any clause in a written contract. So what do you do about them? The first rule for success in handling unwritten rules is to accept that you aren't going to be able to ignore them. The second rule is to accept that changing them is possible – but it takes a long time. The third rule is to find out the specific unwritten rules that apply in your organization as quickly as possible – at the employment interview or before, if possible – and then decide if you can tolerate them. You'll probably find that most of them are trivial and unimportant – like wearing a waistcoat or not wearing bright red lipstick. But you may also find that some of them are more important – such as not confronting secretaries who can't type properly or pushing conflict 'under the carpet'. While some of these may not seem important, they are, nevertheless, symptomatic of the culture (*see* **Archaeology – Corporate**) of the organization. Whether you are – or aren't – compatible with that culture will influence your survival rating in that organization as well as what you achieve there. See if you can identify some of your organization's unwritten rules. Write them down – you'll be surprised by what they cover. While you're at it why don't you see if you can identify what your own unwritten rules are. Write them down, make a list. Then challenge each of them, one by one. Make your mind up about whether they're worth keeping or whether they've outgrown their usefulness.

The new boy who didn't know the dress code.

If the surveys are to be believed then most of you don't take all of the holiday or vacation time that you're due. When you do get away it's often with a mobile phone or the portable computer still linking you to the office. But getting away from it all, taking a break, is an important strand in your strategy for organizational survival. Do it well and you should return refreshed and reinvigorated with a new perspective on all of those persistent problems – as well as being back in touch with your family. Don't do it or do it badly and you'll find yourself sliding further down the slippery slope that leads to increasing stress levels, diminishing ability, ill health and family problems.

So why don't you take all your vacation time? After all, you've earned it. The answers to this question are as diverse and various as the flowers in May. However, they do start to make some sort of sense when you take a look at the sorts of people who don't use all of their vacation time. These fall into three general groups:

1 **The deluded:** these people don't take all their vacation allowance because:
   – they think they are indispensable, or
   – because they don't trust other people to do it when they aren't there to tell them how to.

2 **The compelled:** in this second group are those who don't take all their vacation allowance because:
   – they think it earns them brownie points, or
   – they are too scared to take holiday – because of an oncoming crisis or survival situation.

3 **The driven:** this third group contains those who don't take all their vacation allowance because they've set themselves performance standards which are far too high and, consequently, find it difficult, if not impossible, to let go.

The non-vacationing tendencies of all of these groups are often exploited by bad bosses (*see* **Bosses – Not So Good**; **Bosses – Terrible**) who will use manipulation, coercion, domination and bullying to keep you at the office (*see* **Influence – or Power?**; **Dominance**; **Bullying**). A good boss, however, is different. For he or she will quickly spot a vacation avoider and then work hard to get him or her out of the office when vacation time comes around (*see* **Bosses – Good**).

By now, you've probably worked out which of these groups your co-workers fall into. But what about you? Do you avoid taking all of your holiday allowance? If the answer is 'yes' then it's time you did something about it. Not taking breaks, working late and long – all of this doesn't really earn you brownie points – it just shows that either you're trying to do too much or that the way that you work is either inefficient or ineffective (*see* **Efficiency and Effectiveness**). Surprisingly, getting your holiday right for you and your family isn't an easy task. It takes real skill and ability. But it is a project that's worth working on (*see* **Projects**). You'll have to select the holiday that will suit you and your family, plan it, budget for it and then do it. But all of these are skills that you already use at work. So why not, for a change, use them to get yourself a *good* vacation?

HOW NOT TO No. 10: MOTIVATION AND PERFORMANCE
The ways and means of bad motivation

- ■ Overload people, give them too much to do.
- ■ Make sure that they haven't enough time to do their work properly.
- ■ Make them accountable for their actions, but don't give them any control over the how and when of those actions.
- ■ Give rewards that are insufficient or meagre.
- ■ Increase isolations, limit on-the-job relationships.
- ■ Don't bother about equality, be unfair.
- ■ Put them under the sort of pressure that means they'll skip procedures or bend rules.

VINDICTIVENESS

Being vindictive entails taking revenge upon others for past wrongs, hurts or slights. You do this when you are trying to achieve some sort of recompense or retribution. You're getting your own back. The way things are in organizations, suffering a hurt, wrong or slight is a common experience. It makes little difference whether that wrong is real – or imagined, inflicted with malicious intent – or with casual carelessness. For your hurt and discomfort provided the drive for you to be vindictive.

There are very, very few of you who have not felt this need to right past wrongs. The reasons why you feel that are astonishingly diverse – a list would encompass all of human experience. For some of you, the original 'wrong' might have been so traumatic that the remainder of your life becomes a battle to right that wrong. But, for most of you, the original hurt becomes buried beneath the dust and debris of your everyday lives, either from choice or as a result of emotional torpor. When this happens you run the risk that, when you least expect it, that original hurt will spring forth. It will then move both your feelings and your actions in ways that are not only mysterious but also unpredictable.

So what should you do when you suffer the cuts and blows of another's actions? The first and most important thing is to accept that it's both valid and reasonable to feel hurt. After all, you are human and a part of being so is to feel hurt when others, whether intentionally or not, act against you. The second thing to do is to find someone to talk to about it – a friend, lover, mentor or colleague. This needs to be someone who is both trustworthy and a good listener (*see* **Secrets**; **Listening**). The third and last thing to do is to be patient with yourself. After all, you have been damaged – even though you can't see the cuts and bruises – and all wounds take time to heal. You'll also find that time will bring perspective to your hurt and may even give you the opportunity to right that wrong – assuming that you still want to.

WAVES, SMILES AND FROWNS

When you communicate with other people you usually use words – words that are spoken or written (*see* **Yakkity-Yak**; **Write Words**). But that isn't the only way that you send messages to those around you in your organization. For in those informal one-to-one conversations that dominate your communications most of what you say is said by your body and its movements. You wave, point, smile and frown. You gesture with your hands, fold your arms, scratch your nose, pull your ears, cross your legs and lean towards – or away from – the people that you're talking to. The clothes that you wear, the way you do your hair, the make-up, jewellery and watches that you wear all send messages to the people around you. These 'non-verbal' ways of your communication are called your 'body language'. The power of this language is considerable. It dominates your face-to-face communications, particularly those that involve feelings and emotions. Most of your facial expressions are about expressing those emotions and can provide as much as half of the 'meaning' of any face-to-face communication. But these facial expressions, gestures and movements don't just act on their own – they complement, supplement and add emphasis to the words that you speak. Being able to use and understand this body language is an important skill. Without it you are blind to a major and significant part of the messages that those around you send. With it you are able to read and respond to the whole – rather than just a part – of those messages.

The range of uses that you put your body language to is wide and diverse. You use a gesture to repeat or underline a spoken message – as when you point while saying 'This way, please'. You use body language in ways that contradict, substitute for or complement your spoken words. You also use body language on its own. In a conversation you will use single nods, eye movement and posture changes to indicate that you're listening. You'll also use double or triple nods and other posture positions to indicate that *you* want to say something now. By now, there should be little doubt in your mind about the potential contribution of body language to your survival rating. Body language can give you answers to questions that you dare not ask and answers to questions that you wouldn't get spoken answers to if you did ask them. Using it and using it well can make a considerable contribution to your survival rating.

WE'RE GOING TO HAVE TO LET YOU GO

When you hear these words it almost always means that your relationship with one particular organization is about to come to an abrupt end. The words used are, of course, a euphemism. The harsher, more offensive phrase that it's standing in for is the one that says 'You're sacked'. The reasons for this can be diverse and various. You may have fallen foul of a dominant manager, the company may be closing down or laying people off in response to a downturn in trade or downsizing (*see* **Downsizing**). It may be that your department may be being transferred – to somewhere where labour is cheaper – and you may be unwilling to go with it for family reasons. The role that you carry out may be about to be 'out-sourced' or just 'phased-out'. Your departure may be one of many or one on its own and the way that you're given the news may be careful and considerate or vengeful and tinged with glee. Either way, it makes little difference to what you now need to do.

For what now matters is that you move the focus of your efforts – from working for that organization – to working for and looking after yourself. Most organizations recognize this. They operate a 'here's-your-pay-check-now-go-and-clear-your-desk' termination policy that, on the surface, seems brutal and uncaring. But, in reality, it's actually realistic. Under these circumstances, staying to work your notice out does nobody any good – least of all the people that you work with. Being terminated in that way also gives you the chance to get mad – justifiably so. But that anger – which could be used to create havoc within your former employers' organization – is better used to boost you into another job and another orbit.

The way things are these days getting terminated – or sacked – is getting to be a fact of life. Coping with this starts early – before it happens. You need to face the fact that it could – and probably will – happen to you. You need to do that *now* – not just before you think that it might be going to happen. Once you've done that then you need to take a good hard look at the following pointers – all of which are aimed at helping you to survive the sack. If you've already been sacked then you need to make reading *and acting on* these pointers your immediate top priority.

1 Get Real

Get your head around that fact that the organization that you're currently working for is *very* unlikely to be the one you retire from. Take a good hard look at it – ask yourself what it's doing for you. If you look hard enough you might even see that it's one of those organizations that wants your work more than it wants your loyalty. If you've already been terminated then you need to face that brutal fact face-to-face. It's unfair, unreasonable and may even have given you grounds to take them to the courts – but it isn't going to go away.

2 Share

You need to share what's happening or what you think might happen with your partner or – if you don't have one – with a good friend. Ask them to help you work things through, to identify your options, to find information about your choices and – above all – to support you.

3 Re-invent yourself

Now you need to convert yourself from being pension investor to a brand '*you*', from a good steady administrator to a brilliant change manager, from a 'has-been' to a 'one-who's-time-has-now-come'. If this sounds like marketing or even low quality bull, then remember that if you can't see this in yourself how can you expect potential employers to? (*see* **Re-invention**).

4 Rewrite and polish your résumé or cv

This needs to happen *now* – it's too late when you get the news. Get it into shape, rewrite it so that it shouts out what your skills are, what you're known for and what your personal mission statement is and – if you've yet to be terminated – upgrade it every 90 days (*see* **Résumés and Other Stories**).

> '*Don't compromise your-self, honey. You're all you've got.*'
>
> Janis Joplin

5 Network, network, network

Almost all the good jobs don't get advertised. They get filled by personal contact, by word-of-mouth. So, from this moment on, treat every contact you have as a potential job-creating situation – in other words, get out there and *network*, *network* and *network* (*see* **Networking**).

WHAT MAKES US WORK THE WAY WE DO?

If there's one subject in the study of organizations that people are guaranteed *not* to agree about it's the one that focuses on what it is that makes us do – or not do – what we do at work. As a result, this subject – motivation – has had volumes written about it. The views and theories expressed in these run from the academic to the pragmatic and the real to the surreal. The aim of all of this is to try and find out what it is that makes some people work or perform better than others. You will be pleased to read, however, that it is *not* the aim of this section to add to that pile. Rather, its aim is much simpler and much more pragmatic: it's to identify those key motivational factors that will make a positive contribution to your survival rating.

Motives are stimulating. They induce you to act in certain ways. They give purpose or direction to your behaviour. In your workplace, the motives that are most significant in their action on you are about your ego, security, curiosity and financial position. When all of these are brought together in an integrated and balanced way then the result – usually – is that you are a 'happy bunny'. But when they get out of balance or act in opposition to each other the result is unhappiness, resentment and hostility or to put it another way – an unhappy and often angry bunny.

But, as is so with many things in life, it's often not what you do that counts but the way that you do it or with whom you do it. The freedom of choice that your organization gives you about these factors is limited. You don't, usually, have a choice about who you work with and the way that you do what you do will be limited and controlled by the rules and regulations of your organization. But don't give up. For the word 'supportive' is a key one here. It's also one that's crucial to your survival. For if you see that what is happening to you as being supportive – that is contributing to your sense of who you are and what you're worth – then happiness is close. Good managers know this, bad managers don't care.

Whistle-blowing – or the act of exposing an irregularity, crime or injustice within an organization – is getting to be quite a popular activity. It's almost an everyday event for us to read in our newspapers or see and hear on our news channels about events that one organization or another would rather that we didn't know about (*see* **Secrets**). These can be about almost anything. Corruption, sleaze, crimes, takeover plans, the sudden departures of senior executives (*see* **We're Going To Have To Let You Go**), plant closures, secret new products, tax evasion, misuse of public funds and the sexual peccadilloes of public figures – all of these have been and will continue to be the subject of what is called 'whistle-blowing'. By and large, whistle-blowing comes in two varieties. It can be public and open – as when an individual stands up and makes public what they consider to be a wrong – or covert and hidden – as in the 'Deep Throat' of the Watergate affair or the copy of a sensitive document sent anonymously to a newspaper. The initial reaction of the whistle-blown organization is, however, always the same. Put simply, it is denial, denial and denial – irrespective of the who, how and what of the whistle-blowing. It's also denial that can be followed by counterattacks, harassment and bullying (*see* **Vindictiveness**; **Harrassment**; **Bullying**) – all directed at the whistle-blower.

If you're thinking about whistle-blowing on your organization you should be very clear about the fact that whistle-blowing – and particularly public whistle-blowing – is seen as breaking *all* the rules. There are no exceptions to this. It doesn't matter whether your organization is public or private, profit making or public service. Nor does it matter whether you're whistle-blowing about something that's illegal or unethical, sharp commercial practice or discriminatory. The response is always the same; the sky, as Chicken Lickin' once said, will fall on you – and from a great height. It follows, therefore, that any act of whistle-blowing is an act of courage (*see* **Courage**).

It's also one that should only be undertaken with care and after you've gone through all the following steps:

1 Make sure that you've got your facts right – not just 'maybe' right, but absolutely squeaky-clean right.

2 Don't rely on just one incident, get several examples.

3 Take a good hard look at your motives. There's no room for malice or getting-your-own-back here, nor is there space for political subversion.

You and your facts have to be objective, factual and free from any suggestion of hidden motives.

4 Check out what you've got with somebody outside your organization – somebody who is trustworthy and reliable, someone who won't blow the whistle on you (*see* **Betrayal**).

5 Get them to validate or reject your perspective on the data you've collected. After all, you may be getting hot under the collar about something that's really quite minor or has been publicly acknowledged – and accepted – for a long time.

6 This is *the* difficult one. Now you have to decide if you are – or aren't – going to talk to somebody in your organization about what you've collected. Before you take this decision you really ought to think hard about the what and why of your whistle-blowing. If you have a family or a partner, talk to them about what you feel you need to do. If you've a trade or labour union, talk to them – and listen, really listen, to what they all say.

7 If you decide to go the 'silent' route – that is you aren't going to talk to someone in your organization – then you have to choose how you're going to do your whistle-blowing. Your choice lies between doing it openly or doing it covertly.

8 If you do it covertly bear in mind that you stand a good chance of being unmasked. Remember also that when that happens your organization will say, just before they sack you (*see* **We're Going To Have To Let You Go**), that you should have talked to them and, if you had done, they would have explained it all to you – all of which is designed to make you look bad.

9 If you do approach your organization one of two things will happen. You'll get either a positive response or a negative one. Both of these will, in their own way, be surprising. Be aware that, while there are some organizations who are able to accept and be constructive about this sort of criticism, the evidence is that they are in a minority. Also recognize that some organizations still believe that your contract of employment with them gives them the right to harass and bully you. If this happens get yourself a good lawyer or the backing of your union.

10 Take care of yourself (*see* **Caring**; **Winding Up and Winding Down**).

WHO CARES?

Being careless is the opposite of being careful. You say that someone is careless when they do or say something without due thought about its consequences. But this isn't necessarily an act of deliberate choice. On the contrary, it's usually a 'sin of omission' – rather than one of commission. It happens when you fail to predict the link between your actions and the end result – because you're abstracted or distracted.

But your carelessness can also take other forms. You can be careless because you choose to be. You can choose to be careless towards your co-workers because you dislike them or because you wish to take revenge for real or imagined past wrongs (*see* **Vindictiveness**). You act in this way when you – as a physically fit and able driver – park in a bay reserved for disabled drivers or when you choose not to tell your co-workers about something that's important to them. This sort of behaviour is careless because you make a deliberate choice to act without care for others (*see* **Caring**). It's surprisingly common in organizations. It usually happens when people become driven by self interest, the need to dominate others or the lust for power – and then act without care in order to achieve those ends (*see* **Bosses – Not So Good; Bosses – Terrible; Tall Poppies**).

For most of you, however, your attention is focused on how you can limit the results of this sort of behaviour in others. So what can you do? The answer lies in being the opposite, in being *careful* – rather than careless – and doing so as often as you can. By doing this you'll neutralize the effects of carelessness and you'll limit its ability to damage or destroy the things that make your organization bearable and sometimes enjoyable. Being careful reinforces the sharing and trust that teams need (*see* **Teams**). It provides a foundation for your relationships – ones based on spontaneity, honesty and openness – and it helps you to delight your customers. Chosen carelessness changes people – from happy to sad and from committed to 'don't care'. So take care – of yourself and those around you.

WINDING UP AND WINDING DOWN

Getting wound-up, or stressed, is getting to be a regular, often daily, workplace experience for most of you. Stress appears when the demands of your job become excessive. It raises its ugly head when you try to battle on but find it difficult to do that because of illness, family demands or lack of support and training. It enters your life when your workplace becomes awash with the tides and undercurrents of envy, aggression (*see* **Aggression**) and tension. Surveys tell us that the top ten of the stress hit list are:

1 Frequent interruptions
2 Deadlines
3 Poor communication (*see* **Communication**)
4 Limited support
5 Bad bosses (*see* **Bosses – Not So Good; Bosses – Terrible**)
6 Too many meetings (*see* **Meetings**)
7 Office politics (*see* **Office Politics**)
8 Change (*see* **Change**)
9 Not having enough of the right information (*see* **Decisions**)
10 E-mails, e-mails and more e-mails (*see* **E-mail**)

But being stressed is different from working hard. Stress is your reaction to *excessive* pressure. You become stressed when the pressures of your job overshoot your ability to cope with them. What happens then is that your body kicks-in with their normal reactions to physical threat or danger. You breathe quicker, your heart-rate speeds up, you sweat, have butterflies in the stomach and suffer from a dry mouth or throat. But these are meant to be short term 'get-me-out-of-here' reactions. When they stay with you other reactions appear – headaches, muscle tension in the neck and shoulders, migraine, dizziness and skin rashes or allergies. You become constantly – rather than occasionally – irritable, you lie awake at night worrying about things, you find it difficult to make decisions and, worst of all, your sense of humour disappears (*see* **Laughter**).

Winding down, or getting destressed, starts when you decide to take charge of the situation that's causing your stress. This involves taking stock of what you're trying to do, checking out just how long you're spending on each of your tasks. When you do that you'll probably find that you've been carrying an excessive workload or trying to do jobs that you've not been trained for (*see* **Training**). What you do now is key to the success of your mission to destress yourself. For to reduce your stress level you must now:

■ Eliminate work that it's unreasonable to expect you to do. Talk to your boss about this – he or she may not realize that you're coming in early, missing lunch *and* staying late.

■ Prioritize your work load – daily – and use the back burner for the low priority stuff. Use job lists to keep track of where you are.

■ Delegate routine, low skill, chores to other people.

■ Concentrate your efforts on stuff that gives the highest return (*see* **As, Bs and Cs**).

■ Anticipate – as far as you can – the peaks and troughs of your work load – and plan for them (*see* **Planning**).

■ Learn to say no – don't let other people bully you (*see* **Bullying**) or dump on you (*see* **Delegation**).

■ Find a quiet space where you can work uninterrupted. If there isn't one, nag your boss into providing one (*see* **Quiet**).

■ Don't take work home – work is for work and home is for being with your friends, family or partner.

■ Use relaxation and meditation techniques – to help you keep your cool (*see* **Relaxez-Vous**).

■ Get fit and eat well – but not to excess (*see* **Staying Healthy**).

Stay cool.

Almost all of you learnt to talk before you learnt to write. As a result, most of you talk far more than you write. But, as you know, both of these play key – but different – roles in the way that you communicate in your organization. At first glance, it's easier to see the similarities – rather than the differences – between them. You use them both to pass on information, express your feelings and exert influence or power and they both have conventions or rules about their structures and use.

But when you look at them in more detail the differences begin to emerge. For example, when you write, you tend to use more words, but fewer personal words or references than when you talk. They – writing and talking – are also organized differently. For example, a written text will contain paragraphs, topic sentences and other structural elements. These give the reader signs about the structure and logic of the text. Speech, however, rarely has these. When you talk, you can start – and then restart, switch direction, hesitate and then ignore the rules of grammar. Your talk is influenced by its context and supported by the movements of your body, your gestures and your facial expressions – none of which influence your written words (*see* **Waves, Smiles and Frowns**). You learnt to talk informally, at your mother's knee, while you're taught to read and write in the classroom.

All of these – and other differences – mean that you use talking and writing in different ways and for different reasons. But the written word still makes a valuable contribution to your communication (*see* **Communication**). Because of this it's important to get the right spin on the why, how and when of your writing.

Getting these right will add to your survival rating and help you to use your writing when you need to:

- have a record of what's been said or done;
- be formal;
- be distant from the immediate reactions of the person you're writing to;
- send the same message to several people.

The Xerox or electro-photographic copying machine was invented in the late 1940s. It rapidly became the 'must have' for every office – worldwide. Soon bosses were telling their secretaries to 'make me a Xerox' of a document rather than to 'make me a photocopy' of it. In this way the brand name Xerox travelled the same route as Hoover had decades before. That is, in everyday speech, to Xerox something became code for the act of photocopying it.

So, given that even Xerox hasn't yet mastered the art of photocopying people and hence halving all our workloads, where does all this get you? The answer lies in the fact that, in the hustle and bustle of the twenty-first century workplace, you are all copiers – and not just of documents! For when you see somebody with a good product that sells or a good idea, wheeze or twist that works, the temptation to Xerox or copy that product, idea or twist is enormous. The days when NIH or 'Not-Invented-Here' was the standard, knee-jerk response to other people's innovations are long gone. Now it's a 'me-2' world that you live in. Successful products are cloned with a rapidity that was unthinkable a decade ago and the market place advantage that follows from their introduction is as short lived as the May Fly. So when you see somebody succeeding in your organization the temptation is for you to emulate or imitate them. But all that this 'me-2ing' produces is hundreds and hundreds of counterfeits. For the courage, sparkle or zest that led to the original success is gone, the cutting edge that led to its original impact is history. All that is left is a hollow shell bereft of its early promise. What this means is that if you really think 'xeroxing' or 'me-2ing' is a good way to raise your organizational survival rating – then you're in for a shock! But let's not throw the baby out with the bathwater – for there is a way that me-2ing can help you. But in order to do that it has to change, become something else, a something else that is 'me-2 *plus*'. For 'me-2 *plus*' can take an idea A that works in one place and, with unique and special changes and enhancements, turn it into idea A++. Doing this is just as creative as creating the original idea. It's also a logical extension of the process of accumulating and consolidating small increments of change and improvement that led to that original breakthrough idea or product. It's also a good way of increasing your survival rating.

You spend a lot of time making those yakkity-yak noises – talking. Most – though not all – of this is done with other people. However, there are also occasions when you talk to – rather than with – inanimate objects, such as trees or computers – or animals, such as cats or dogs. Sometimes, you might even talk to yourself. For most of you, talking is one of those taken-for-granted actions – much like walking, hearing or seeing. You've learnt to do it instinctively, often without much prior thought or preparation. As such, much of what you say is colloquial; that is it uses, by choice, 'common speech' rather than formal or 'elevated' speech. The sorts of thing that go on in your brain when you talk are only partially understood. But when you do it you are able to persuade (*see* **Persuasion**), debate (*see* **Dialogues and Discussions**), influence, instruct, inform, even seduce each other. Much, but by no means all, of this talking takes place in conversations (*see* **Conversations**), conversations that are conducted either face-to-face or over the telephone. When you talk face-to-face – and do it well – your words and movements begin to fall into a sort of 'dance' with each other. The rhythm, volume, speech rate and pitch of your talking, your gestures and 'micro-movements' – all of these become interwoven, harmonized. Good speakers know this, so do bonus-winning salesmen.

But when you talk on the telephone, things are different. For then you are like a talker in the dark; you're visually cut off from the person that you are talking to. In these conversations there are no gestures, grimaces or smiles to tell you what they think of what you are saying; there are no nods or turns of the head that tell you that they can hear you. But, like talking in the dark, a telephone conversation has its good points. For when you talk to others on the telephone you are as invisible to them as the laws of physics allow you to be. The listener cannot see you. As a consequence, you can talk to them as you lie soaking in your bath or curled up in your bed. You can scratch yourself, pick your nose, kick off your shoes, glance at a newspaper or the TV – and all of this is hidden from them. But this concealment can be penetrated. For those who hear you are free of the distractions and deceits of your body language (*see* **Waves, Smiles and Frowns**). They focus on your voice; they 'read' its tone or pitch, they hear the way that you do or don't hesitate, the pauses in or between your sentences, the speed or volume of your speech. And, as is so in your face-to-face conversations, they make use of these to deduce how you are feeling or what your attitude is towards them or the subject under discussion. Their and your ability to pick up and interpret these complex aural signals is quite considerable. Nevertheless, talking on the telephone is as near as most of you will get to being blind.

You can – and do – talk about almost anything. Most of the time, however, you talk about what interests you personally. But, whatever you talk about and whoever you talk to, you also face a choice when you talk. For your talk can be truly yakkity-yak. It can be trivial, persistent, unfocused. But it can also be about sharing your feelings, experiences, hopes, desires and fears. When you talk to share your plans for the future, your regrets about the past and your anxieties about the present – then you're *really* talking (*see* **Your Future**). For this sort of talking enables you to build relationships, dispel tensions and resolve conflicts. Talking well can increase your survival rating.

'Yes . . . of course . . . I'm working on it now . . . but I'm very busy . . . can't see my desk for paper.'

YOU'RE IN – OR YOU'RE OUT

Whether you're part of the 'in-crowd' or outside it is quite important. For when you're in – you feel good, you 'belong'. When you're out – you feel bad, undervalued, rejected. This business of being in – or out – is one that happens quite a lot. It happens in the workplace, when you are – or aren't – drawn into the informal ad hoc discussions that take place at the coffee machine or the water cooler or when you are – or aren't – invited to join that exciting new working party (*see* **Secondments**). These 'in-groups', cliques or sets come about for two reasons: firstly, because they answer your need to belong, and, secondly, because they give you the feeling that you are 'different' because you are a member of an 'in-group'. Most, but not all, of these 'in-groups' are informal, almost ad hoc, in nature. But that doesn't mean that they don't carry out a valuable function. For they act as the gossip marketplace (*see* **Gossip**), they are where you debate – albeit informally – important issues (*see* **Dialogues and Discussions**). They can keep you informed about what's happening, who said what and why this or that should – or shouldn't happen. But at their worst – and worst is often more common than best when it comes to 'in-groups' – they are exclusive sets of individuals who lay claim to a sort of 'supreme' authority about social status, pecking order (*see* **Pecking Order**), what's right for the organization, etc. and do so without just reason.

But let's not forget that organizations themselves are 'in-groups'. Before joining your organization you are interviewed or tested (*see* **Testing Times**). Your invitation to join this organization followed if, and only if, you passed these tests. Then, and only then, were you judged 'fit' to become a part of that 'in-group' and to be fully exposed to its culture. Later, you'll probably be invited to join other formal and informal 'in-groups' – groups of people who share job titles or responsibilities with you, groups of people who have a common aim or objective (*see* **Teams**). But no matter how far you rise in these 'in-groups', you'll only survive if you remember what it was like to be outside – in the 'out-group'.

The future is made of much the same stuff as today – except that it's arranged differently. This means that if you're going to have any success in checking out *your* future then you've got to start by accepting two fundamentals. These are that it – your future – will, whether you like it or not:

■ be different from your past, and

■ will involve lots and lots and lots of change.

So if you're hoping for security, certainty and a steady, serene voyage towards your pension – then forget it! Accepting these fundamentals – and their consequences – is important. Until you've done it you'll not be ready to move on to the next two key issues. These are just as important as the two above – but not so easy to believe or accept. For these tell you that your future can be, if you really want it to be:

■ much more in your control than you currently think it is, and

■ more fun that you're having right now.

Not easy to accept, are they? They fly in the face of your past experience, they turn your hard earned and battle scarred cynicism on its head. But all you're being asked to do, at this stage, is to accept that they *might* be possible. For possible they are – if you *really* want them to be. Here are some actions that'll help you to build *your* future:

Discover *you*

This ain't easy. You're going to have to break yourself out of the world of off-the-shelf, pre-packaged and pre-labelled people and become the you that you really are – the one that can move mountains. It ain't quick. Once you've started you'll find that you're on a journey that will take you the rest of your life – one that you may never finish (*see* **Re-invention**). But it is worthwhile.

Be optimistic

Smiling is *good*. When you use the muscles of your face to smile – even when you're not happy – it actually causes the chemicals that make you feel optimistic and more relaxed to be released in your brain. It's a self fulfilling action – like being happy (*see* **Laughter**).

Seek out challenges

Make them real challenges – the 'I'm-not-sure-I-can-do-this' sort and stretch yourself to meet them.

Affirm yourself

Affirm your own right to be on this planet at this time, affirm your right to be the person that you are, affirm the skills, abilities and creativity that are *you* (*see* **Self Stuff**).

Helicopter up

Be open-hearted, learn to see the whole picture – rather than just the few pixels that are in front of your nose. You'll be surprised what you can see from up there! You might even see the shining towers of your own future in the far distance.

Learn to learn

Learning to learn is *good*. It helps you to understand and cope with the world of your organization. What happens when you learn is that you ratchet-up your skills, expertise and abilities. You enhance both the width and depth of your competencies (*see* **Training**).

Find a mentor

A mentor is somebody you can talk to, who's seen all – or most of it – before and will help you to find your way through the traps and tricks of life in the organization to your future. A mentor is, at one and the same time, a friend and an experienced and trusted counsellor. Getting yourself one will increase your survival rating by leaps and bounds.

Be curious

Curiosity, they say, killed the cat. But all that it'll kill for you is your old ways of looking at things. Get on the Web, read all those books that you meant to but haven't found time for, every week read a magazine that you wouldn't usually read – one that's outside your usual interests, go on vacation to somewhere really different. Get – and stay – curious.

zany (´zeɪnɪ), adj. Comically idiotic, crazily ridiculous.

'There may not be a reason for saying something until after you have said it.'

Edward de Bono

'Abolish Celery.'
Graffiti

'The good news you cannot refuse. The bad news is there is no news.'

N.S. Engel

'Sometimes a cigar is just a cigar.'
Sigmund Freud

'Say No to an important person.'
Graffiti

'I have seen the truth and it doesn't make sense.'
Unknown

'Reality is a collective illusion.'
Graffiti

'If I can't dance I don't want to be part of your revolution.'
Emma Goldman

'There ain't no rules around here! We're trying to accomplish something!'
Thomas Edison

'The future belongs to the discontented.'
Advert for medical equipment

'Ready, fire, aim.'
Anon

'First things first, second things never.'
Shirley Conran

'The meek shall inherit the earth . . . if you don't mind.'
Graffiti

'I am here to live out loud.'
Emile Zola

'Two leaps per chasm is fatal.'
Chinese proverb

'Truth is the safest lie.'
Anon

'Reason argues – Intuition leaps.'

Anon

'Take work as a game and enjoy it.'

Bhagwan Shree Rajneesh

'It's clear to me that when we function smoothly as a group, our differences and gripes become irrelevant, but we do not lose our distinctness. It's transformational. The very substance that was an irritant becomes a note in a harmonious chord.'

David Chadwick

'It is better to have lived one day as a tiger than a thousand years as a sheep.'

Alison Hargreaves (died on K2, August 1995)

'What I have learned is that people become motivated when you guide them to the source of their own power.'

Anita Roddick

'We are often trapped by the images we hold of ourselves.'

Gareth Morgan

'Waste no more time arguing what a good man should be. Be one.'

Marcus Aurelius

'No company can be successful, in the long run anyway, if profits are its principal goal.'

Ricardo Semler

'Change breeds opportunity.'

Robert Waterman

'Shortcuts always cause problems.'

Philip B. Crosby

'It is about a search, too, for daily meaning as well as daily bread, for recognition as well as cash, for astonishment rather than torpor, for a sort of life rather than a Monday through Friday sort of dying.'

Studs Terkel

'Life is not a dress rehearsal.'
Rose Tremain

ACKNOWLEDGEMENTS

Special thanks are due to Katie Roden, Editorial Director of the Teach Yourself series at Hodder & Stoughton – for seeing in this book what others hadn't seen and then being willing to take the risk – and to my partner Linda Baguley – for the inspiration and for putting up with all those dawn starts and lost weekends. Particular mention should also be made of the contributions – albeit indirect – of Pat Howe, Jackie Keyes, Paul Lennon, Alison Richardson and Sue Roberts – all of whom are 'tall poppies' and know why their names are here. Thanks also to Peter Stockbridge for the great cartoons, and to Jill Birch for all the work she put into the process of getting this book to you, its reader.

Phil Baguley
Brighton, England
Spring 2001

TEACH YOURSELF

NEGOTIATING

Phil Baguley

Teach Yourself Negotiating is an important book for all professionals. The need to negotiate effectively exists at all levels in all organizations. Whether you are dealing with colleagues, suppliers or customers you need to be able to negotiate – and do it well.

A book you cannot afford to be without, *Teach Yourself Negotiating*:

- shows you how to prepare for, carry out and complete your negotiations
- helps you decide what strategies and tactics to use
- illustrates how to use the bargaining process to generate a successful outcome
- guides you to a successful implemention of that outcome
- provides a checklist for assessing your own negotiating skills.

Phil Baguley is an experienced business writer and lecturer. He has held senior management roles in multinational corporations and has also worked as a management consultant in the UK and Europe.

TEACH YOURSELF

PROJECT MANAGEMENT

Phil Baguley

Teach Yourself Project Management is a practical introduction to the craft of project management. With diagrams, useful ideas, appropriate methods, check lists and tools it explains and illustrates the what, why, when and how of this form of management. The ultimate guide for all who wish to develop the skills of effective project management.

The book shows you how to:

- manage, plan and organize your project from start to finish
- create an effective project team
- estimate and manage your project budgets
- solve problems, and monitor and control the activities of your project.

Phil Baguley is an experienced business writer and lecturer. He has held senior management roles in multinational corporations and worked as a management consultant in the UK and Europe.

TEACH YOURSELF

BUSINESS PRESENTATIONS

Angela Murray

Giving a presentation can be a daunting and nerve-racking experience, even for a regular presenter – what can you do to give yourself confidence and ensure success? *Teach Yourself Business Presentations* provides the answer. From defining the brief to post-presentation analysis, the book supplies a step-by-step guide to the skills and techniques needed to deliver an effective, engaging presentation.

Team presentations, presentations to colleagues, informative and persuasive presentations – appropriate techniques are considered for these and many more. Throughout the book imagination, innovation and creativity are all actively encouraged.

Covered in the book:

- strategic planning – defining and analysing the brief
- planning and research
- creativity
- communication skills
- audio-visual aids
- 'presentation etiquette'and personal presentation
- analysing performance.

An easy-to-read guide, full of hints and tips, this book provides support and guidance for the novice, and fresh ideas for the more experienced.

Angela Murray is a freelance Business Consultant specializing in marketing communication and presentation skills.

TEACH YOURSELF

IMAGINATIVE MARKETING

J. Jonathan Gabay

Powerful marketing campaigns are based on original thinking and creative planning. *Teach Yourself Imaginative Marketing* concentrates on the engine which drives successful marketing – imagination. Revealing many profitable tips and secrets to help you target, brand and sell your enterprise whilst generating provocative publicity, this book will keep you three steps ahead of the competition.

The book:

- covers the key marketing areas of sales, advertising, PR and branding
- concentrates on the dynamic 'imaginative' side of marketing
- is easy to follow with useful activities and exercises
- includes a comprehensive 'jargon buster' section
- is suitable for anyone working in or studying marketing.

Completely up-to-date, ready for the cut-and-thrust world of marketing beyond the millennium, this book is indispensable for anyone who wants their business careers to succeed and continue to breed success.

J. Jonathan Gabay, a Course Director at the Chartered Institute of Marketing, has worked for some of the world's biggest advertising agencies and on some of the best-known marketing brands.